# The Business of Relationships

# The Business of Relationships

## Creating Enterprise Success With China

Joan Turley

BUSINESS EXPERT PRESS

*Leader in applied, concise business books*

First published in 2022 by
Business Expert Press, LLC
222 East 46th Street, New York, NY 10017
www.businessexpertpress.com

ISBN-13: 978-1-63742-187-1 (paperback)
ISBN-13: 978-1-63742-188-8 (e-book)

Business Expert Press International Business Collection

First edition: 2022

10 9 8 7 6 5 4 3 2 1

# Description

Understanding how relationships work is the most significant aid to creating success with China. Adding a culturally aware set of relationship-building skills to your existing business offer opens doors in China and facilitates meaningful trade, longevity in business relationships, and lasting success with this business culture. Drawing on intercultural expertise and practical experience of relating to China, this book will guide you at every step of the business process to show how your skills can be enhanced by the relationship knowledge it offers. Succinct, yet offering great depth of insight, this book is the ultimate primer and reference guide to creating enterprise success with this relationship-centric business culture.

This book will explain the principles behind China's devotion to relationships and why relationship networks constitute actual business collateral. It will further demonstrate why you will be effective and successful in this business culture if you show the requisite skills for relationship handling. You will also find expert counsel, in this book, on how to skillfully blend your existing business skills in negotiation, deal-making, governance, leadership, and intellectual property protection, with a China-adapted style of conducting relationships. The knowledge offered by this text will allow you to fuse these skills in a way that signals that you are trustworthy, capable, accessible, and relatable, thereby facilitating success and establishing trust.

## Keywords

China success; relationship handling; people-centric culture; China fluency; China and mutual benefit; creating trust with China; stakeholder management; metacognition as a China skill; China and leadership; enterprise success; deal-making China style; avoiding conflict in China; China and IPR management; resolving conflicts with China; successful deal making with China; successful negotiation with China; handling setbacks with China; handling adversity with China; accountability and China; China adapted business plans and goals

# Contents

*Introduction* ....................................................................................... ix

Chapter 1   People Skills, Partnerships, and Relationship
Management Skills ............................................................1

Chapter 2   Communicating for Success.................................................13

Chapter 3   Negotiating for Longevity and Success............................21

Chapter 4   Making Deals That Work and Last in China..................29

Chapter 5   Protect the Relationship to Protect the Deal ....................39

Chapter 6   Repairing and Rebuilding the Relationship:
Conflict Resolution, China Style .....................................49

Chapter 7   Creating and Maintaining Success With China .............61

*Demonstrating China Fluency: Key Dos and Don'ts* .................................69

*Conclusion: Creating Mutual Benefit and Shared Reputation*..................77

*References*................................................................................................79

*About the Author*.....................................................................................81

*Index* .....................................................................................................83

# Introduction

The goal of this book is to identify the essential nature of success in trading with China. For this, I have drawn on a decade of personal and professional experience of creating trade, partnerships, and successful links with both the private and the public sector. It was with great ease and conviction that I identified relationships as the central tenet of any template for creating success with this business culture; this is because, from my earliest business interactions, I observed that relationships are what matter to China. They are also what make Chinese businesspeople feel secure enough to partner and to trade. Relationships that are solid, well made, and heavily invested in, are what it takes to gain trust and loyalty with Chinese businesspeople.

Before explaining the crucial significance of relationships in China, I feel it is important to provide you, the reader, as the next generation of businesspeople to succeed and thrive in China, with the motivation for the task of exploring China's approach to relationships. I will do this by giving you both a context, and a rationale, for *why* you should invest in understanding relationships in the Chinese business model.

In doing this, I am aware that we, in the West, would rarely identify relationships as the central tenet of business creation within our own business model. I am, therefore, requesting a significant shift from you, so that you can create real and enduring success for your enterprise with China. To encourage you in this shift, I would like to introduce you to key Chinese values, principles, and protocols, which will truly help you understand why relationships lie so profoundly at the heart of all success with this business culture.

Nearly one-fifth of all humanity lives in China (BBC News 2021). It is perhaps supremely fortunate, then, that China is a culture that values people as both the reason and purpose behind any, and all, interaction and endeavor. It is a people-centric culture with a supremely people-centric approach to doing business. In China, children learn by observing how relationships underpin and create order in the lives of those around them; they see the networks of relationships and how these facilitate progress in good times, as well as in times of adversity.

Children are made aware, when they are still quite young, of the enormous import of their role in the Greater Collective. The word for person in the Chinese language is *Yi Ge Ren* (一个人) and is defined as a unit of collective humanity. The concept is a cherished one, imbued and instilled in Chinese people from earliest infancy. A Chinese child learns emotional intelligence, which, in China, correlates with relationship skills, alongside all other learning. This induction into the crucial importance of relationships is considered fundamental and transmitted early to the Chinese child. This is essential in a world where the success of an individual, his family, town, province, et cetera will thrive only if that individual develops a proficiency in character judgment as well as a strong facility for relationship-building and maintenance. The child is further encouraged to develop an intuitive and sophisticated level of attention to relationships in all their forms.

In a relationship-centric culture *mianzi* (面子) or public *face*, that is to say, the image, dignity, and reputation you hold in your world is everything. In relationship-centric cultures, therefore, reputation becomes a significant life asset—arduously built yet easily lost, if not diligently maintained.

Alongside this crucial notion of relationship primacy and dedication to the Collective, the Chinese study and assimilate writers and thinkers whose wisdom is considered perennial such as Lao-Tse, Confucius, and the writers of the Bing fa wisdom texts (Turley 2010). The principles at the heart of these texts emphasize the building of character within the individual. They do not, however, place this emphasis on character for the purposes of creating individualism, rugged independence, or personal advantage, as is often the case in Western business culture. Rather, they focus on the self/other integration which emphasizes the Collective and the responsibility to play one's role well within this Collective.

The emphasis, as you would expect in a relationship-conscious society, is on good character and on associating with good characters. It further emphasizes the building of strong relationships as well as mindfulness of how these can bring reputation to both the Collective and the individual. The critical premise in Chinese thinking is that: the individual thrives if the collective thrives; this is a premise sometimes echoed by the revered thinkers in Chinese history (Turley 2010)

So, the Chinese place huge emphasis on cultivating soundness of character, skills, and on reputation building, while seeking to combine this with astuteness of judgment. The belief is that it is this blend of skills and qualities that will bring a good public face to you and to all those on whose behalf you carry reputation.

In the West, our interactions are primarily filtered through our relationship to the self. In China, these are filtered through "the other" and the collective reputation of one's social fabric. This framework requires a heightened sensitivity to the interconnectedness of one's reputation with that of others. As such, it tends to automatically engender a sustained vigilance to the well-being of the relationship, the creation of mutual benefit, and the desire for shared, harmonious outcomes.

How does this translate in the real business world? Here, too, China retains its relationship-centric framework, values, and criteria. For the Chinese, openings and deals come wrapped in relationships and the responsibility to assess all such opportunities for their reputation-building contribution. This is an entirely pragmatic approach when we remember that in this culture *face* is life itself. Such an approach requires a shared, uninterrupted commitment to preserving the most polished and unbroken contribution of a harmonious self/other relationship to the world.

So, motives, intentions, character, and dedication to shared reputation are all examined in the early stages of the relationship process within Chinese business dialogue. The great practical thinkers in Chinese history like Confucius focused on character, self/other integration, and judgment as the fundamental route maps to success (Csikszentmihalyi 2020). So, the exchanges that occur in early business dialogue are designed to identify within prospective partners: good character, soundness of intention, the presence of a win/win mindset, adroitness in creating joint reputation, and the will to make these goals the primary business objective. Without the desire for mutual benefit, the Chinese believe, there is simply no deal to be done.

Therefore, relationship-centric cultures take their time and can appear to be less goal-oriented and process-driven than other business cultures, such that of the West. The Chinese allow relationships to organically define their business model and give the latter time to develop. They expect these models to fluidly follow the rhythm of the evolving relationship and see external business pressures and the creation of outcomes as secondary to the building strength of the relationship bonds.

Furthermore, the Chinese expect relationships to be the markers for progress in all business concepts. In particular, they expect that when assessing such concepts as integrity, accountability, partnership, and progress, the true determiners lie in the health of the business relationship and not merely in commercial definitions of success criteria.

In a relationship-centric culture, therefore, there is a huge emphasis on what is happening underneath the business dialogue and interactions. China concerns itself with the values, motivations, intentions, behavior, and character of those who would partner with it because in such a *face*-conscious culture, this is the most pragmatic, intelligent, and effective business approach possible. Once you have explored and, hopefully embraced, the skills needed to relate well to these expectations, you are then in a strong position to adapt your business in a way that allows you to thrive in China.

The additional skills needed, while relational in nature, make sound business sense in a culture where relationships, not process, engender and protect success. With some adroit intercultural adaptation, your skills will attract China and create the success with this thriving business culture that you seek. Let us begin to examine relationships in more detail, now that we have a cultural context for them, and guide you through the process of becoming China-adapted in your handling of business relationships, thereby ensuring success for your enterprise or endeavor.

Relationships matter enormously in China. They are based in trust as well as a willingness to create, and preserve, shared reputation. They affect, influence, and, in many cases, determine the outcome of our business journey. They are prevalent and influential in all aspects of our dealings in China from the earliest, exploratory stages of business dialogue, through to negotiation and deal-making and finally implementation, governance, and project management. They are fundamental to all success, and they are the measure of success. They overcome obstacles, repair damage, and protect all business outcomes, deals, and profits.

It is precisely because of the crucial nature of relationships in China's business world that this book will take a relational approach to your success with China. It will also act as a pragmatic guide to deploying relationship fluency and finesse, alongside other business success skills such as negotiating, people-handling, deal-making, and project management.

In doing so, it will ensure that the collective deployment of your business skills and talents are China-adapted, thereby facilitating success.

In order to arrive at this goal, I must first explain the specific ways in which relationships drive success in this business climate. I will also show the cultural roots underpinning the huge import China accords to relationships within their business culture. Finally, I will demonstrate how China-adapted relationship skills, when coupled with developed communication and people skills, and accompanied by negotiating flair and deal-making prowess, create success with China. In doing so, I will provide not just a success template, but the means to sustain and protect this success; this will include the means to future-proof it and protect it from adversity or reversals.

China-adapted relationship skills build strong and lasting partnerships, facilitate negotiations, and act as robust guarantors and protectors of both the partnership and the deal. It is to relationships that the Chinese turn to solve any point of conflict or discord by repairing what they see as the true, causal element in any such situation—a rupture in the underlying relationship itself.

Furthermore, relationships protect the business parameters of all that is shared in partnerships: intellectual property, project management skills, technology, and talent. More than this, they ensure mutual accountability and mutual benefit, which makes the Chinese feel safe to partner and trade.

At this juncture, most Westerners legitimately ask how relationships, which they have always regarded as firmly within the business "soft skills" area, can possibly be such potent determinants of success in pragmatic business areas like negotiation, project management, intellectual property protection, and deal-making. For the West, used to an increasingly transactional model of business, this is a stretch and an extremely uncomfortable one, at that. It is also, however, a fundamental one, which we must make, if we are to succeed with China. It could be summed up as follows: "In the West, we have a relationship because we are doing good business." Whereas, in China: "We are doing good business specifically, and primarily, because we have first developed a strong relationship." Bridging these two definitions is both an opportunity and a challenge.

The opportunity is to become China-adapted in the application of your business skills and talents, thereby ensuring success and longevity of trade. The challenge is to increase your current level of emphasis on relationships significantly, to the point where sustained investment in relationships is your primary goal within the business process. Lasting success with China demands no less than this, of all who engage in trade with her.

This book will give you all the tools to bridge the process-driven business model favored by the West and the cherished relationship-centric model favored by China. It is an increasingly sophisticated adaptation that is required, as the Chinese themselves continue to embrace and significantly adapt to Western business styles and practices, also. Over the last years, fueled by global success, China has embraced greater levels of sophistication in relating to Western markets, trading practices, and styles of business governance, all the while successfully emulating much of what it sees.

Fundamentally, however, despite surface accommodations of Western business styles with their more transactional preferences for operating in business, China's core model for the cocreation of success rests firmly on character, trust, shared reputation, and the search for mutual benefit. Since such values rarely define, motivate, or underpin Western business models and behaviors, to the same extent, we can see the work that lies ahead of us. It may appear a complex task, but it is not. It does, however, require strong intention, commitment, and motivation, for this is not a matter of the superficial matching of business etiquettes or cultural protocols.

This is, rather, about harmonizing two different approaches to business skills, goals, and outcomes and, more fundamentally, about the "modus operandi" through which we achieve those business goals and outcomes. It is also about releasing preconceptions and fixed, monocultural notions of business methods. Instead, it is about being open to the huge benefits of a mediated blend of two distinct business models in the service of your own enterprise success with China.

To encourage us in the task, let us pause and consider the significant potential rewards for your business or venture, of engaging successfully with the established trading superpower that is contemporary China.

China's rise to becoming a truly global trading superpower has been both brilliantly strategic and meteoric. Deng Xiaoping's efforts to open up China economically only began with his accession to power in 1978 and the introduction of the socialist market economy (Chen 2001). Many China commentators have simplified this notion using the phrase "to get rich is glorious" (ibid.). Although often attributed to Deng, the original source has never been established (*LA Times* 2004). This simplification does, however, try to capture the economic progress of this time. It represented a critical turning point in that it provided the moral and ideological weight to the notion that China could now boldly welcome investment, redefine its profile as a consumer, and embrace the expansion of its knowledge and trading status, as well as its innovation and partnership boundaries.

This is precisely what China set about doing with huge gusto, admirable strategic thinking, and demonstrable effectiveness. In doing so, China welcomed in significant foreign direct investment (Chen 2001), learned to partner Western enterprises, and became versed in, and sensitive to, our business models, developed management science, and preferred models of corporate governance.

All the while, China was moving speedily, and inexorably, from being the "world's workshop" to a sought-after trading destination and, ultimately, to becoming a leading investor and principal on the world's trading stage. While all of this was occurring, China's own appetites were changing and a new class of consumer was embracing the chance to spend, after a prevailing ideology of saving. Disposable income rises, along with more indulgent and benevolent political attitudes to spending, gradually made China a major market for health care, beauty products, luxury items, fashion, including haute couture, luxury cars, yachts, and personal accessories (Chua 2012). It is both certain, and inevitable, that other sectors will follow.

Meanwhile, though, China's own dedication to innovation and continual investment in research and development, coupled with its willingness to learn from the knowledge bank of its Western partners, has promoted exponential growth and standing; China has now become a major exporter through firms like Huawei in telecommunications and Haier in white goods (Chakravarthy and Yau 2016).

Moreover, the extent to which China now partners or leads ventures and industry initiatives within Western countries, from publishing to nuclear energy, is now also extensive. Its influence within ASEAN (Xiao 2009), as well as its influence through its own ambitious Belt and Road trade initiative now make China's standing indisputable. China will continue to use this standing to grow its reputation as a trading partner, a commercial market, and a highly solicited trading destination.

Furthermore, since Chinese business culture is one which always plans for the medium and long term, and uses the same word, *wēijī* (危机) both for crisis and opportunity, it is important to understand that China will protect these new advances, and always seek to establish longevity in its successes. This means that China will continue to offer opportunities to partner, sell, share, and innovate with Western businesses for an exceptionally long time to come, since this is precisely what China likes and seeks: stability, continuity, and loyalty in how, and with whom, it trades. All of this means that China is a highly promising choice for your enterprise success, both in the short and longer term.

It further means that, if well made, your relationships will ensure longevity of trade and a level of customer retention which we can only dream of, in our increasingly transactional, and fickle, Western business climate.

Assuming you accept that both your skills and business offer would benefit from being China-adapted, your next consideration is whether you fully believe that the service, goods, product suite, research content, or area of expertise you possess is something that China currently needs, lacks, and wants. Providing your business opportunity audit is carried out within a careful due diligence and reveals that there is real value to the Chinese market in terms of what you have to offer, you are ready to prepare your China entry.

Now comes the big decision: Are you willing to do what it takes to trade with a relationship-centric culture, which will demand that your people-handling skills are placed at the core of everything you do in business? At this point, you must also ask yourself if you are ready to engage in a business model where each significant stage of development, from initial discussion to negotiation and deal-making, through to partnership and project management, must be preceded by an ever-greater investment in the relationships you are building.

Central to this consideration is a clear understanding of what we mean by investment in relationships, for what successful trade with China asks of us is a real investment of self, time, energy, commitment, and proofs of goodwill. This equates with the intention to put relationships at the core of the entire business process and to undertake to create, under all circumstances, clear mutual benefit, and shared reputation.

If, as I hope, the chance to participate in this person-centric, loyal, and flourishing business model is sufficiently attractive to your business, then this book will guide you through the exciting understandings, insights, and openness required for the China adaptation of your individual business skills, permitting you to flourish in this market.

Few people remain unchanged through the process of creating and sustaining deep relationships with China and its people-centric business culture. Indeed, a deep trading relationship with China is often reported as fundamentally, and significantly, one which enhances everyone's business and cultural viewpoints as well as skills set (Chen 2001). This business journey offers the chance, if we are willing to embrace it, to become our own able and gifted mediator, capable of creating significant levels of mutual benefit and profit with the new economic superpower that is China.

## Creating Relationships That Matter With China

Culturally, the Chinese make sense of the world and create structure, as well as order, through relationships. The paradigm for relating successfully, while creating social order and harmony, was established through Confucian teaching (Csikszentmihalyi 2020) and acts as a core model for all relationship categories, including business.

The main paradigm for relating well is built on five constant basic relationships. These, in turn, enshrine the Confucian golden behavioral and attitudinal standard (ibid.), which we will discuss in more detail later on. These core relationships are parent and child; husband and wife; elder sibling and junior sibling; elder friend and junior friend; and ruler and subject. These rules or Li (礼) contain universal and timeless wisdom about how relationships can be managed and should be both respected and protected.

At the core of the application of these rules is the golden rule that we do only unto others what we would wish for ourselves. Meant pragmatically, this rule advocates for situations in which mutual respect, reciprocity, and mutual benefit become guiding concepts. The aim of the broader relationship paradigm is to infuse a sense of respect into our primary relationships so as to ensure that the process of self/other integration is truly successful and creates positive outcomes for all. This would, in turn, allow for all organizations, sectors, governments, and models of business and society to function harmoniously. For as Confucius said: "let the ruler be a ruler, the subject a subject, the father a father, and the son a son" (Chen 2001).

A fundamental prerequisite to any success requires an understanding of this relational model and its cultural roots. One must also appreciate how this relationship model manifests, in real terms, in the behaviors of Chinese business interlocutors. It is not a "soft skill" as we view it in the West. It is the core skill required to allow other business talents to shine. It is the template for how business is done and the facilitator, as well as modus operandi, of all progress. Moreover, it is the protector of all progress made and a key component of the preferred Chinese way to manage any success created.

It behooves us, therefore, to view the awareness, understanding and mastery of this relational model as central to our China-adapted portfolio of business skills. We would also benefit greatly from viewing this, in turn, as being fundamental to how we show respect in China, earn trust, and provide proof of worthiness as a reputation partner. Without such a disposition, any success in China will be grueling to achieve, hard to maintain, and extremely likely to stall or even fail.

Let us begin, therefore, to deconstruct this relational model with a view to participating respectfully, capably, and successfully within this business culture. If we do this, we ensure our projects, goal, aims, and aspirations can all be successfully met within our dealings with China.

Confucius spoke about the five relationships that are key to harmony and successful functioning (ibid.). All of these are close, reciprocal, and respectful of one's role within the relationship paradigm.

They also display wisdom through irrevocably linking the successful handling of relationships and power with maintaining balance and producing positive outcomes. The Chinese relate fundamentally in relationships to these Confucian guidelines for creating mutual benefit and success. This is because they wholeheartedly subscribe to the underlying principle that, if relationships are in balance and in a state of harmony, then success for all concerned is inevitable.

Crucially, none of these relationship models apply to people who are strangers at arm's length or outside of your personal connection network, nor do they apply to those who are considered beyond the realms of your social obligations. A crucial imperative, therefore, in succeeding with China is to move from the status of untrusted outsider to trusted partner. We achieve this by behaving, from the off, in ways which are meaningful, well-intentioned, sincere, and nonshallow. This behavior must apply to all those with whom you would make successful business dealings, regardless of status or degrees of influence. It is then imperative to treat prospective partners as people with whom you wish to make deep connections; with whom you are happy to create mutual advantage and obligation; as well as valued networking relationships.

Connection is paramount in China. The Chinese emphasis on people, and collective success, marks such connection out as a pragmatic and essential prerequisite to dialogue and negotiations. In a world where people matter phenomenally, and all success models are fundamentally relationship-centric, levels of connection and skills in people-handling become accurate predictors of success. They also act as proofs of character and evidence of a talent for sustaining relationships and reputation which the Chinese value enormously in anyone they trade with, manage, partner, or buy from.

So, how do we move from the level of outsider or untrusted stranger to trusted business interlocutor and potential business friend? The process is really a journey into trust for the Chinese and it begins with a due diligence on the character and intention of prospective business interlocutors.

If profits were achieved in a way, or at a speed, which proved harmful to relationships, reputation, or cherished business contact networks, they would not be desirable to the Chinese. Indeed, to protect relationships and reputation, the Chinese are frequently more relaxed about the speed of generating profit. Instead, China's business culture prefers to focus more on the organic development of the project and optimizing core relationships. These relationships, in turn, act as a facilitator and highly reliable medium, as well as long-term indicators of profitability.

The logic the Chinese hold is that if all elements are taken care of equally, including and especially relationships, the ultimate result will be a healthy one in terms of outcomes and profits. Most significantly of all for the Chinese, this outcome will have been achieved in a way that preserves reputation. Since reputation constitutes collateral of primary import in this relationship-centric culture, enduring success can only be guaranteed by protecting reputation in business, since it is the true guarantor of profits.

There is an important point of Confucian training behind this notion of correct business attitudes. Confucian core values, which serve as the primary success guidelines for most Chinese businesspeople, are rooted in respect for authority, beneficence, nonmaleficence, and justice (Csikszentmihalyi 2020). At the core of these ideals is the concept of mutual benefit and being worthy of a task or a role, a role that is of critical value if one is to create collective success and harmony.

Therefore, Confucian thinking suggests, one's best and most efficient self must be brought to the task, project, or role in hand. From this, success is guaranteed because the goal is worthy, the behavior is ethical, and the underlying relationships, which are the carriers of all true success, are well made and valued.

If this method fails then, within the Confucian paradigm, it means that the goal is worthy of retention, but the method needs to be adjusted.

Confucius believed that all social and business relationships create mutual obligations (Chen 2001). If these are observed, then we can flourish and succeed while building harmony. The Confucian value of playing one's individual part well, while being vigilant and admirable in our public conduct, is at the core of good business practice in a relationship-centric culture. This is evident in the Chinese dedication to, and obsession with, relationship, face and reputation both in business and in life.

Confucius advocates mutually beneficial conduct in the leadership of people and execution of tasks, ventures, and projects (Turley 2012). To achieve this, he puts forward two templates for behavior in relationship to self and other. First, he encourages us to reach for the superior man—our best self—and to bring that to bear in how we undertake our role and play our part. Second, as leaders, we must participate in models that are as interested in people and reputation, as they are in profits and gain: "The rule of virtue can be compared to the Pole Star which commands the homage of the multitude of stars without leaving its place" (Confucius 1979).

The Bing fa texts, such as the *Art of War* are often quoted by Western management science (McNeilly 2011), and primarily offer templates for creating gains through strategic prowess. Unlike the authors of such texts, Confucius places the emphasis on proving ourselves worthy of the success, prominence, profits, and reputation we seek to create (Csikszentmihalyi 2020). The emphasis is on character; this is the template that has made its way into Chinese business. It is also the reason why, despite the alignment with Western business practices, which China has engaged in since its "opening up," China continues to put an extensive emphasis on character as a prerequisite to partnership. The establishing of trustworthiness in China remains, and will always remain, a core prelude to any business engagement.

The West, unused to due diligence processes that are quite so extensive in the area of character, or to having to provide proofs of trust in order to engage in business dealings, find it more challenging to participate in a model where trust is such a fundamental prerequisite to trade. Given this, how can Western businesspeople fare well in the crucial early stages of trade with China, where character is so heavily and intensely scrutinized?

First, we need to be willing to participate in this slowly unraveling character audit that is early-stage business in China. Our goal is to signal that we have understand the crucial role of trust and can give clear proofs of faith of our own trustworthiness. The more obvious proofs include keeping in contact, keeping one's word, respecting hierarchy (remembering that China is a vertical business hierarchy), and being sensitive to cultural values and norms. We also need this sensitivity to extend to Chinese preferences in business pace and method, which may be different from our own Western practices.

We will further need to show graciousness when plans change, as they frequently do in the highly organic climate of Chinese business. Indeed, in the words of one Chinese CEO whom I previously interviewed, "the plan cannot chase change" (Turley 2010). This expression captures their firm belief that business is best done by letting the organic process of business dialogue unfold naturally. Relationships become critically important within this paradigm, for it is the health of these very relationships which accommodates the organic unfolding of business processes and deals successfully with change and contingency, where required.

Above all, what China seeks is compelling evidence that we can go beyond surface proofs of faith, significant as these are, toward more China-adapted and deeper proofs of business goodwill and integrity of intention.

Such proofs of faith include showing your understanding of the crucially important status of relationships. You achieve this by proving not only that you put relationships first, but that these lie at the very heart of your business style, goals, and modus operandi, just as they do for the Chinese.

To assess if this is indeed the case, you will be closely watched by your Chinese business interlocutors in terms of how you treat your colleagues in critical situations and demanding business climates. Such contexts include: how you behave in group situations; in public or official gatherings; at moments of media attention; in prolonged negotiations; in business downtime; at the end of tiring days and, especially, in moments of business change and flux.

In all the above, it is important to remember to be modest, invested, caring, collegial, and collectivist. We will discuss more of this vital disposition—and how to acquire it—later in the book. However, for the purposes of building confidence during the initial character due diligence, it is crucial that you signal trust, relationship finesse, modesty, and commitment to public face, reputation, and relationships. This involves bringing a fundamentally people-centric aspect to everything that you do, from the very moment you first engage in business with China.

The early character due diligence starts with these questions: is this person a trustworthy relationship and reputation partner? Remembering Confucian principles, will they do their part? Will they protect my reputation? If, as is the case in China, reputation equals business survival, no business of any import gets done before these basic proofs of good character are fully established, secured, and firmly in place. Once they are in place, however, the real business can begin and will already be off to a truly marvelous start.

# CHAPTER 1

# People Skills, Partnerships, and Relationship Management Skills

## Contrasting East–West Perspectives on Relationships

The building blocks of relationships in China are different to those in the West. Business relationships in the West, operating in what is essentially a process-driven business culture, are propelled by values such as performance, efficiency, shared profit targets, and the willingness to set, and abide by, contractual trading formats and legal partnership obligations.

The trust that we build is almost exclusively based on these performance values: efficiency, accountability, reliability, demonstrable results, and shared return on investment (ROI). Where these elements are not present in Western business relationships, they tend to fail, as they are primarily based on the cognitive trust that emanates from good performance. Nowhere in all of this is there the kind of unconditional loyalty the Chinese expect, one that is present at the time of adversity and demonstrates dedication to shared reputation and a sincere commitment to mutual benefit. The Chinese expect these values to be the hallmark of all worthy business relationships, worthy partnerships, and enduring business success stories.

This is largely because performance is the value that we cherish most in the West, the one which is universally lauded by an entrepreneurial, individualistic business culture, which enshrines its successes within processes and law. Performance, we believe, guarantees profits. Trust within this model, therefore, relies largely on accountability, efficiency, and adherence to contract. Law, within this paradigm, removes any of the true need to cement business dealings into relationships that outlast adversity or weather business setbacks. In a relationship-centric culture conversely, there is a fundamental need to create and sustain business relationships which outlast adversity and weather change in ways which will be flattering to the public reputation of both parties. Moreover, in such a culture, efficiency and performance on their own are not sufficient; it is expected that these will be accompanied by a deep-seated commitment to the interest of the other.

For many people in the West, particularly in the context of business, this sounds like an abstract and very intrusive imperative. Indeed, to Western business sensibilities, this seems both unnecessary and somewhat out of place in the pragmatic forum of business or the ROI and profit-led philosophy of commercial organizations.

In China, however, reputation, face, mutual benefit, and perceived business harmony are the very elements that ensure profits. They are also the factors that drive progress, success, and ROI. So, the roots of how this success is created, nurtured, and protected must go deeper. They must lie in the fusion of competency and compatibility and must always be underpinned by soundness of character.

Once this is in place, the Chinese feel safe to trade and cocreate success. Such success is then celebrated by enshrining it in joint reputation. Joint reputation is, in turn, communicated through public statements of commitment to each other's competencies, character, and behavior; this is achieved through a publicly stated commitment to joint success and mutual benefit.

Let us see how this translates in terms of practical success creation by looking more closely at how good business equals relationships which are well-made. We will further see how, by excelling in relationship building, you can write the optimum script for your enterprise success in China.

## Displaying People Skills

People skills tend to be viewed in the West as a desirable accessory to a more hardcore portfolio of business talents. The somewhat secondary importance of these skills is reflected in the term commonly used to describe them: *soft skills*.

In China, people skills, alongside partnership-building talents and relationship finesse, are all viewed as a primary, if not *the* primary skill set for business success. You do not make it beyond the introductory or exploratory stages of business in China if these are not in place. The Chinese consider levels of skill in these areas to be easily verifiable and set about diligently ascertaining if a prospective potential Western partner possesses them in sufficient depth. They do so, in order to move onto the real definers of business collateral in Chinese business culture: relationship readiness and character strength.

These tests are the ones that will determine your success. In China, *you* are the deal, project, task, goal, and outcome. Your character and your ability to build reputation, show resilience, respect public face, and think collectively are what encourage the Chinese to trade or partner with you.

Significant and enduring success with China relies on us engaging in behavior, communication styles, and decision making, which play well to the Chinese family-based business model. It also involves us embracing collectivist thinking and the creation of shared reputation as the overriding, sustained, and primary goal of our business dealings—from which all other success follows.

Relationships and people skills as well as fluency in cultivating and sustaining partnerships are of paramount importance in China. Such expertise centers around the notion of partnership harmony as a central value from which all meaningful success emanates. The creation of face, therefore, is crucial in a society where reputation is business collateral and where disharmony destroys deals. The creation of successful joint face facilitates success and protects against conflict. There are essentially three core value sets then, which must underpin our relationship skills and will readily convince the Chinese that our business talents are China-adapted.

*Successful relationship handling involves:*

- Putting the health of the business relationship we create at the core of everything we do rather than treating them transactionally, and putting them in a subservient role, secondary to outcomes and processes

- Investing in reputation creation as a primary goal. This is a truly central litmus test for the Chinese. If a prospective partner cannot grasp, and constructively work toward, shared creation of reputation at every stage of the business process, then the Chinese cannot envisage a long-term partnership or trading arrangement. This is because in China, quite simply, reputation is success
- Creating harmony at all stages of the business process

The Chinese dislike conflict, process for the sake of process, transactional relationships, rigidity in business thinking, and public squabbling or disagreement. They also abhor overt, prolonged litigation, since resorting to such litigation is seen as both harmful to relationships and a failure to maintain them successfully. Therefore, they respect reciprocal, consensual relationships where everyone plays their role, respects norms, and works collectively, to maintain face, harmony, and collective reputation.

Conflict resolution, the Chinese passionately believe, would not be required if we respectfully put harmonious relationships as the primary goal of success and trade. For the Chinese, partnerships well-made equal success; relationships well-handled equal avoidance of conflict; reputations successfully managed equal the protection of deals done and longevity of association.

We will now look at how these three core value sets can be incorporated into your business disposition; how they can be reflected in your communication of goals and of your character; how they can be signaled through your negotiation, team making, and governance behavior, and how they can appear to be at the center of all the trading interactions you undertake.

## Making Relationships Central to All That You Do

The business models of the West and China have different tenets, belief sets, and operational frameworks. Fundamentally, the Chinese value set is centered in the belief that, without mutual benefit, enhancement of relationships and reputation, and maintenance of harmony, no deal is worth doing. The most important of these core business concepts to China is the notion of public face and reputation. Your first task, therefore, will be to signal your trustworthiness to the Chinese in a way that resonates with their core definitions of trust, concerning the soundness of your character. To understand how to do this effectively, we must first ask ourselves how the Western and Chinese business models differ, in their emphasis on relationships, as core facilitators of success in partnership.

In the West, we have increasingly moved toward a process-driven, individualistic model of business. While individual autonomy and entrepreneurship have thrived within this paradigm, the critical importance of relationships has tended to be relegated to the soft skills area. In the place of relationships, the Western business model has codified its management structures and governance and created a system of support through law and litigation to guard the parameters of its business processes.

Our energy has gone into becoming exceptionally capable at the core elements of trade, negotiation, contract discussion, and deal-making. Moreover, within this paradigm, we have increasingly integrated a heavy level of recourse to law to protect all stages of progress. Eventual recourse to litigation is also a key component of the model, to be invoked in the event that the business process undergoes unforeseen challenges or fails to deliver the expected outcomes, at the expected rates and within the proscribed time periods.

Our process-centric business model is, for this reason, increasingly referred to as transactional. The transaction counts first and foremost rather than the people we make the transaction with. Of course, within these parameters, we endeavor to show integrity, professionalism, and business courtesy, but we are, nonetheless, governed by process, by rates of progress, by outcomes, and by eventual yields. The concept of ROI is king in the transactional Western business model and it would be increasingly considered unusual to place people or partnership above this, in terms of the core business value or cherished asset.

The Chinese, on the other hand, are not fundamentally transactional in their business culture. Rather, they follow a relationship-centric business culture. What does this mean in real terms? Quite simply, it means that relationships protect, encourage, facilitate, and define the nature of all business deals. As such, any deal that looks profitable but harms the relationship is viewed as fool's gold, since relationship and reputation are the ultimate determiners and protectors of success. Without them, in Chinese thinking, there is no possible longevity to one's current success and future potential success is aborted due to the failed nature of the relationships we have built.

We need, therefore, to acquire a thorough knowledge of how to participate well in relationships in China and create shared reputation. We need these elements to form part of our primary goals and overriding skill sets. Establishing soundness of character, is the true due diligence that the Chinese seek to carry out in the earliest stages of any business process. The thinking is this: if you have a dedication to the business relationship and the requisite skills in creating reputation, when inevitable difficulties arise within your joint project or trade discussions, these will be dealt with effortlessly. This is because challenges can be easily weathered within the context of a strong partnership.

As we have identified previously, the word wēijī (危机) in Mandarin signifies danger or crisis but also opportunity. With strong partnerships, we do not have to dread reversals—we weather them. In the same vein, the Chinese believe that there is also no need to dread deviations from, or setbacks to, our plans and timelines. Having built strong partnerships and solid reputations, contingency can be navigated easily.

The success of this approach was demonstrated during the Asian financial crisis of the 1990s when people and businesses within China lent each other money, acquired companies that were in trouble from each other, hired each other's employees to protect them from redundancy, and, in some cases, merged business offers to ensure mutual support and a record level of speed in emerging from the crisis (Chen 2001).

So how then do we, in the West, signal trustworthiness, given our formation within a more transactional business model, in order to participate sincerely and profitably within the Chinese business culture? First, by reevaluating the priority of relationships in your business value set. It was not so long ago that we, in the West, operated on a model closer to that of the Chinese. The 1990s brought a huge drift toward a more process-driven, transactional way of conducting business (ibid.). So, begin by asking yourself if you, personally, and the enterprise you represent, are happy to commit to doing business with a relationship-centric focus.

Then, consider what people skills, strength of character, and levels of commitment to mutual benefit you can identify within yourself. Also consider and evaluate which aspects of your character can be deployed to signal your suitability and worthiness as a partner, in a business model dominated by face and reputation. Beyond that, it is important to build your cultural awareness in terms of what China-adapted people, reputation, and partnership skills look like and to signal your readiness to embrace these in your business portfolio.

Much of the core values for business behavior in China, despite modernization, are fundamentally Confucian in nature. At the center of these beliefs is the notion that a superior man shows both vigilance in speech and behavior as well as dedication to the collective good in their business conduct (Csikszentmihalyi 2020). This is in marked contrast to the rugged individualism and self-reliance advocated by iconic business leaders in the West. For Confucius, modesty and a people-oriented approach, which seeks to foster group harmony and shared accomplishment, was the ultimate success ideal. This involved, primarily, everyone knowing their part and playing it assiduously. Mutual benefit with success represents the very essence of the template that Confucius promoted—one that is still very present in the minds of our potential Chinese business partners or customers. Embracing this template, we begin by signaling a commitment to mutual benefit, shared reputation, joint face, and the willingness to nurture relationships as the central foundation of our business approach.

In seeking to show commitment to our business relationships with Chinese partners, it is important to deploy curiosity about our potential partners' families and towns. It is helpful to take an interest in their children's education, as well as in their company or organization, since the latter are often treated as an extension of the family unit in China. Enquiring about their city and interests also acts as a huge pillar in the bonding process as it speaks to Chinese core values of connection to family, town, city, organization, and work life. In other words, it speaks to the Chinese network of relationships.

There are other significant ways to bond and promote trust in prospective partners in China. These include showing tolerance to changes of timetabling and extended days; being willing to reveal one's character and looking for ways to harmonize your goals with those of your partners and making accommodations, where possible. All of the above helps to further build and consolidate trust with the Chinese. To move our status from potential to actual trading partner, vendor, or manufacturer in China, we must take every opportunity to go the distance. This will involve earning respect by giving more than you take, giving proof of a flexible disposition and embracing setbacks.

To further demonstrate that you understand how the Chinese like to build partnerships, it is also recommended that you avoid recourse, in the early stages of business, to legal ratification. Such behavior looks like a sign of bad faith and signals poor trust levels in terms of the people behind the deal.

Next, share knowledge without undue suspicion. The Chinese appreciate partners who are willing to advance their knowledge store and knowledge itself is viewed, in China, as a universal value. This is reflected in the Confucian statement: "I transmit rather than I create" (Soetendorp 2008). So, while not recommending a reckless attitude in relation to your intellectual property rights (IPR), it is important to display a knowledge-sharing disposition. This signals good faith toward the partnership you are building and indicates your willingness to increase your partner's knowledge base.

Remember that you are cultivating a deep and long-term relationship, so your willingness to inform and transmit ideas that enlarge the Chinese knowledge store is, in fact, something that the Chinese do automatically and often for a trusted friend colleague or partner.

The goal for work to succeed is to move from the status of *outsider* to someone who is worthy of close business allegiance. Central to achieving this goal is the imperative to build bonds of trust with the Chinese. Indeed, given that we are dealing with a business model that operates on dissimilar values and assumptions to our Western model, the building of trust becomes indispensable.

Building trust can significantly lower the level of what Westerners perceive as irregular or inconsistent behavior in the Chinese. This includes the inscrutable nature of the Chinese often described by the Westerners. It also helps to illuminate the seeming aversion in our Chinese partners to accountability. Trust, in China, encourages not just accountability but transparency in business dealings. This is because once trust is securely built, the Chinese are happy to explain and make visible both their thought process and end goals.

One very enlightened piece of work from Massachusetts Institute of Technology (Chua 2012) suggests that we need to build levels of trust that go beyond the cognitive model, which predominates in Western business, where we trust people based on their accomplishments, skills, and reliability and on the degree to which they are helpful to our goals. This study suggests that a higher level of trust is required for China, one that must include trust from the heart or affective trust. The latter is fostered when successful bonding occurs through the creation of significant levels of empathy, rapport, and engagement.

Combining cognitive and affective trust is what the Chinese do so very well. It is fundamental to their world view and it is this blended approach to trust that allows the Chinese to feel safe to trade, partner, and cooperate (ibid.).

In our Western business model also, trust, character, and business bonding used to play a greater role in our business behavior and decision making. While these instincts were largely abandoned in favor of processes, paradigms, and business checks such as ROI, we still possess them. In China, these skills, rehabilitated and given weightier significance, become huge assets. The trust China is looking for in its partners is twofold: the faith it wishes to have in its partners' skills, accomplishments, delivery abilities, and knowledge capabilities is one element. The other is the trust that emerges from a reassuring analysis of character and the building of successful bonds with prospective partners.

For the Chinese value set, when character is trustworthy and commitment to joint reputation is secured, it is safe to give one's confidence in the knowledge that success will surely follow, given the strength of the business bond that has been established.

Willingness to establish good character in the eyes of the Chinese is what gives us a meaningful edge in China; it is this which opens doors, facilitates timelines, and brings us to the deal-making table. This does, however, take time. Confucius recommended closely observing potential partners for some time before committing to them, as he believed that a man could only dissimilate for a short period and would eventually reveal their character in its entirety and comprehensiveness (Confucius 1979).

It is only at this point, Confucius believed, that one could be certain this individual would play his part well, protect reputation, and be an effective partner in the creation of success with mutual benefit.

This is even more necessary, because China has experienced its fair share of what it calls "briefcase companies." This was a term coined by China to describe the many companies who came to trade in China over the last decades without the requisite business credentials and inadequately underpinned by stakeholders (Chen 2001). These companies were often opportunistic in their business behavior and potentially harmful to the reputation of any prospective Chinese partner. As a result, character due diligence is, a priori, no longer carried out quickly in China. However, if this phase is navigated successfully, the levels of trading opportunity and the longevity of partnerships on offer regularly outstrip what we might see in the West.

To speed up this phase, you must look to the second core value set: the creation of mutual benefit. You might usefully ask yourself what you can do to signal a commitment to this goal and give proofs of your ability to create it. Further, it is helpful to examine how you can display willingness to have mutual benefit as a guiding business principle.

It is not advisable to fabricate such intention and commitment if they do not resonate with your core business values, approach, or behavior. However, it is important to know that commitment to these values is of primordial importance in China; no true or lasting success occurs without such commitment. This is why the assessment of one's values forms such a significant part of the initial evaluation that the Chinese carry out, so thoroughly, on all business partners.

So, assuming you have the intention and motivation: how do you signal this? Essentially, by being the opposite of the *briefcase companies* who are opportunistic, transactional, process-driven, and obsessed with deals and contracts.

Mutual benefit involves a much more holistic approach to trust building; it sees both a strong bond with our partners, as well as the joint responsibility for reputation creation, as goals in and of themselves. These are considered primary goals, from which success will inevitably emanate.

Look, therefore, at what you can do for your Chinese business partner, his town, his family, and his organization. Chinese obligations are wide, constant, and far-ranging from family, to city, to country, and to the reputation of all the above. Take an interest in the well-being of a partner's city and the educational aspirations your partner holds for his children; give credit frequently to your Chinese partner, particularly publicly, for the achievements and progress of your joint trade or partnership. Such actions enhance the reputation and standing of your Chinese partner and demonstrate that you understand his concerns and responsibilities. Take every opportunity to provide public face and add to the reputation of your prospective partners; this means a huge amount in a face-based society where reputation is actual business collateral.

Monitor the health of the relationship constantly. Build it up in person, visit often, keep promises, and only ever use a soft "no," particularly in public. If you cannot acquiesce, avoid overt negation, and give your Chinese interlocutor an exit route, in a manner that saves face. This kind of skill can be quite easily and quickly built and is phenomenally valued in Chinese culture; therefore, it is at a premium. In intercultural terms, these skills are collectively referred to as *cultural metacognition* (Chua 2012), which means simply that we cultivate always a sensitivity to the preferences and cultural norms of the other. It further requires that we commit to constantly testing out our own cultural assumptions in the context of real experience, feedback, and responses from our trading partners.

Such a skill requires an initial shift from us as it means we must move away from being primarily content, process, and outcome based in our business behavior, responses, and interactions. Instead, we need to become truly attentive to our mode of communication and relationship signals.

Furthermore, we need to read, carefully and consistently, both the behavior and responses of our Chinese partners as these are the primary litmus test of business progress. While this may initially appear daunting and time-consuming, it is, in fact, a relatively easy skill to acquire. Furthermore, it has the added advantage of making our business dialogue so much richer, deeper, and more effective. It spares us cultural misunderstandings, prevents business holdups, and it offers effective damage limitation where mistakes are made. Metacognition is the ultimate success skill for China.

This book will help you build this reflex so that you can become your own cultural mediator and read your Chinese business partners accurately and with understanding and empathy. Indeed, it will become as easy and gratifying to build success with China, as it currently is with markets and cultures more familiar to you. The results are worth the effort. Indeed, not only will gains occur in the short term but given the Chinese propensity for loyalty, they will yield long-term rewards. With the skills described above, it is possible to create a mutually beneficial, profitable business relationship, one that is blessed with the kind of loyalty and longevity of association, which is increasingly uncommon in Western business culture.

# CHAPTER 2

# Communicating for Success

## Contrasting East/West Communication Norms

In the following chapter, I now propose a template for communication with China built on what I have observed as both effective and successful in cementing great business relationships. Before I do this, however, it feels important to give some context on how the Chinese view communication. The context for communication in China is primarily a relational one; in this model, communication contributes to and fits around the needs of the relationship, not the reverse. In the West, the context for communication is the transmission of clarity in ideas and it is the efficient and effective transmission of ideas that constitutes the primary role of communication in our business culture.

This is a significant contrast and affects the way our communication models relate to each other. This contrast, perhaps more than any other factor, is responsible for many intercultural communication problems, clashes, and misunderstandings. It can be avoided if we become aware and remain conscious of our partners' cultural attitudes to communication and the specific import it holds for them.

If, like the Chinese, we are determined to bond through language, preserve relationships and create harmony and public dignity through each negotiation, discussion, and business communication, then our approach to what we say must be carefully filtered. Tone becomes incredibly important and the manner of our interactions should always avoid robustness, overtly direct negotiation, and any perceived dominance of the business discourse by any one party.

Soft communication, as well as the seeking of consensus, become paramount in a communication model where each interaction or exchange is meant to build the bond between prospective partners and their projects. In this model, any discourse that is of a public nature becomes one in which the relationship is built up, accorded reputation, and publicly celebrated.

Public communication, in China, is even handed, equal, reputation-conscious, and harmony-building. Within the Chinese model, it is a chance to add public face and depth to a building relationship that has already been significantly invested in, in private. The Chinese expect such delicacy and relationship-sensitive communication styles in all who hope to trade and partner with them. The Chinese themselves deploy this sensitivity of communication styles as a priority and in a sustained manner.

The expectation of sensitivity and finesse in handling communication on the part of the Chinese extends to the legal counsel of those who advise their future partners. It further extends to how future partners access such legal counsel and the way in which legal discussions are communicated. The Chinese expect sensitivity in the building of contractual structures around potential deals and the handling of specific points of contention. It is crucial, once again, that law is not perceived as adversarial, overly robust, or hard edged as none of these communication styles favor public face and reputation enhancement. Nor do these styles forge the kind of trust, entente, and harmony that the Chinese need to accompany legal interventions in any deal-making situation or long-term partnership negotiation.

For us in the West, conversely, it is the *idea* that is king. Communication is about expressing clarity of vision, terms of engagement, goals, requirements, contract obligations, and expected ROI. We value directness, robustness, frank exchanges, direct negotiations, and hard-won, and often robustly contested, legal contracts and frameworks.

The parameters of communication in the West highlight the things that matter to us: progress, transparency, achieving goals, and securing deals through law and clarity. Such objectives inform the way we deploy our time, energy, resources, and expenditure to achieve our goals. Therefore, robust dialogue, saving time, progressing the deal, wrapping it in a watertight legal expression, and securing desired outcomes, as well as significant and robust levels of ROI, are what drive the communication style we adopt, overtly or covertly, in Western business.

We also feel particularly proud if we have set the tone, pace, and rhythm of the negotiating process through the manner of our presentation, the robustness of our negotiation tactics, and our directness in communicating ideas. Indeed, these are viewed as the being the hallmark of a seasoned business operator and able negotiator. Where problems arise during such communications, we use frankness to iron out difficulties and reach a consensus of a kind. We assign to lawyers the task of recording the fine detail in a way that ensures all parties are held to the terms of the deal under threat of legal sanction for any contraventions of the said terms.

None of this constitutes acceptable communication or interaction for the Chinese, because it does not feel respectful to the relationship. Nor does it contain the kind of consensus, flexibility, or fluidity that the Chinese consider essential to maintaining harmonious business relationships. Indeed, it does not feel like the kind of communication style required for building partnership, promoting deep exchanges, establishing bonds that create business trust, or cementing long-term relationships. Most of all, it does not represent, for the Chinese, the kind of language that is conducive to creating deals that are balanced, respectful, and steeped in mutual benefit.

Western business communication styles, on the contrary, feel much more aligned to combat, tests, and conflict. This mode of communication feels combative to the Chinese as well as adversarial and impolite in its directness. It constitutes, therefore, a threat to public face and trustworthy long-term partnership. As such, it feels like an impoverished mode of exchange and the kind of communication that would harm reputation, face, and public standing.

In a people-centric culture, reputation is allied to every single communication and therefore every single communication matters. As such, all communications must proclaim shared harmony, good face, desire for consensus, shared reputation, respectful exchange of ideas, and a communication style rooted in respect, mutual benefit, and trust. With the understanding of these contrasting frameworks between China and the West in place, let us move to seeing how you can mediate these contrasts with increasing ease and fluency to facilitate enterprise success for your business or organization.

# Developing Culturally Adapted Communication Skills

Our communications skills are chiefly informed by the values and language norms of our culture. China is no exception. While most Western cultures, with some variance in degree, operate in a low-context language framework with language content being the main carrier of meaning, China operates on a different language framework and is high context. In this culture, one infers meaning not from the content only but from a host of factors that include tone, gesture, facial expressions, social context, suggestions, and general inference.

Largely these contrasts emanate from two distinctly diverse approaches to what communication means, as well as how it relates to role, identity, and public face. Once again, we will look at this topic in a relational framework because, in China, the primary role, contribution, and context for communications *is* a relational one. First, let us consider the fundamental value and import that communications hold for the West and how this contrasts with China. This will make it much easier to embrace the task of adapting our communication style to make it effective for our China dealings.

As we saw earlier, within our Western culture, communications exist primarily for the transmission and exchange of ideas. Our primary concern, therefore, is for clarity, precision, and the accurate conveyance of these ideas. As such, what is said, and the precision with which it is said, matters more than how the information is received.

We pride ourselves on directness, forthright expression, robust description of our needs and requirements, and the frank communication, where necessary, of clarification, criticism, or conditionality. All of this we see as amounting to transparency, since plain speak is our Holy Grail and unvarnished communication the very stuff of good business practice and clear audit trails. Hence our increasing fondness in the West for recourse, whenever we encounter difficulties in business, to litigation. Law is the ultimate low-context environment, where everything is about the stated content, rather than the context of the exchange or a concern for how the material or contract communication will be experienced by the receiver.

In China, communication is about the preservation of harmony, the creation and maintenance of good relations, the observation of role in status, the giving and receiving of faith and respect, the maintenance of reputation, the sharing of ideas, and the creation of organic progress. Therefore, no communication, big or small, is ever undertaken without the following considerations: What is my role in relation to this group? What is the status of the person I am addressing? How can I give face to all present through my mode of communication? How can I preserve my face through this communication? How can I share ideas to promote harmony? How can I phrase what I wish to communicate in a way that will cause no offense to those present?

It is for this reason that Chinese communications are slow, very measured, and contain frequent pauses and silences as the latter allow for reflection and careful, harmony-producing styles of exchange.

So, what are the core rules and how can we adapt them to our personal communication styles, while remaining authentic in how we communicate? Happily, most of these require merely a shift in register and intensity that can sit comfortably alongside our own personal communication style.

First, since relationship preservation is our goal, we need to embrace a more indirect style of communication. We can use styles of questioning that are softer, do not require blunt yes or no answers, frame questions as exploration, use oral rather than written communications, avoid overt criticism, and start with affirming or positive phrases.

All of the above avoid loss of face and putting your Chinese interlocutor on the spot. This is never a comfortable feeling for the Chinese since public competence and reputation is of paramount importance to the individual their family, their organization, their town, province et cetera.

In China, the individual carries the public face and reputation of all those they are connected to; it matters profoundly to them. In business, it is the difference between success and failure. So, it is crucial to behave in a way that allows your Chinese partners face and kudos by communicating to preserve relationship and build reputation.

Avoid gregariousness, establish credentials early by situating yourself within networks, be modest in your speech, avoid gesticulations, excessive emotion or anger, and you will immediately make your interlocutor feel safe to share ideas and create progress.

It is also crucial to avoid culturally laden idioms and jokes. Many of our business terms in the West relate to sports or to cultural practices and idiosyncrasies that cannot readily be understood by China. This leaves your business partners exposed in business discussions and negotiations. China does not have the luxury of direct or blunt questioning at such moments where clarification is required and will often instead have recourse to silence, rather than embarrassing our business partners with a "what do you mean by that?" type of question.

So, we need to communicate in a measured, sensitive, harmony-producing way. For this to become automatic, we simply need to filter what we are saying through the prism of: will the communication, statement, or question that I am about to offer, harm, or hamper relations and dialogue at this table?

In many ways, we already use a filter in the West for our communication, except we are primarily concerned not with harming or hampering the relationship, but rather harming or hampering progress and success. Note the vastly different and very telling contrast in emphasis. In China, however, where relationships are the ultimate progress and success facilitators, arbiters, and protectors, we need to ensure that we convey messages in a gentle way. If criticism needs to be expressed, do so gently and privately. Make criticism structured and solution-based; allow an exit for the person you are criticizing; soften the delivery by references to any past errors of your own or past shortcomings.

The Chinese adore people who are genuinely humble, self-deprecating, and above all, collectivist in their thinking, communication, and responses. Instead of the Western emphasis on "I" the Chinese value those who express the collective will of their business team, organization, and company. They also expect praise and responsibility to be collective and for there to be minimal differentiation of the individual and the group. Therefore, be mindful of the deference levels you show colleagues.

Another good strategy is to express opinions in collective terms. When accepting praise, do so sparingly in regard to self, deflecting it rather to the wider team, as this is the Chinese way. This more harmoniously matches

Chinese understanding of good character in terms of personal humility and willingness to be a team player.

All of this resonates with the Confucian notion that everyone is playing their role well, which, in turn, makes the Whole, successful, harmonious and reputation-worthy (Confucius 1979); this is an important factor in terms of how we address different interlocutors. China has a vertical hierarchy. In business, this means that how we address a CEO is not in the same register as the one we would employ to a more junior member of the team. Factors of age, seniority, public profile, and status are all considered in Chinese business culture and combine to form the context for appropriate communication.

Some general rules, applied sincerely, will keep us safe here:

- Always defer to the social status of your interlocutor; if uncertain, assume it is higher.
- Always use a respectful tone and pause before responding.
- Always respect age and seniority in the vertical business structure.
- When speaking of self, always use reserve and humility in tone.
- Always keep emotions in check and private; these are rarely expressed in Chinese business culture.
- In moments of high stress, stay silent or use very measured communications.
- Avoid absolute statements, overt judgments, or harsh comments and make sure that everyone ends the conversation in a harmonious state.
- Listen very carefully.
- Use silences to reflect.
- Avoid sudden, uncontrolled gestures, theatrical or dramatic presentation styles or statements.
- Deal in facts and precise business scenarios.
- Avoid the use of the conditional (what would be) as the Chinese do not have this tense or frame things in this manner.
- If you have to say no, make its expression sensitive and equivocal.

In addition to the aforementioned, when agreeing matters with Chinese interlocutors, examine the "yes" you have been given since the Chinese are reticent to offer any form of direct "no"; remember that "yes" in China can range from being a mere expression of interest to a firm acceptance of terms under discussion. If there is a great deal of qualification, rumination or procrastination take the "yes" you have received from the Chinese as soft. In such instances, make allowances and proceed accordingly, paying attention to the relationship to help you regain ground and move forward.

Do try to make it easy for the Chinese to show you the stumbling blocks of any potential agreement in a way that is non embarrassing to the general face of those present; handle such stumbling blocks and challenges carefully and sensitively.

Above all, achieving a communication style that truly serves you in China is about practicing cultural accommodation, that is finding ways to blend the communication style that makes your interlocutor feel safe, with one that makes you feel authentic and successfully heard.

We will see how these communication styles can be further deployed, in action, as we continue to build your active portfolio of effective communication skills for China within the context of negotiation. You may be confident that, with the right insights, understandings, and strategies, a China-adapted communication style is within your grasp. Practicing the tools given here, and in the following chapter on negotiation, will help you achieve this effective communication style successfully.

# CHAPTER 3

# Negotiating for Longevity and Success

## Contrasting East/West Attitudes to Negotiation

As with all other business skills, we will excel in demonstrating our negotiating prowess once we know how to adapt this skill to Chinese business culture. To do this, we need to first understand the context for negotiating in China.

The Chinese see negotiation as an exercise in the respectful exchange of ideas, methods, and business acumen toward a common objective and shared goal. This approach provides mutual and benefit and enhanced reputation for both parties. The Chinese relish the process of defining objectives; considering interesting and strategic routes to these objectives and finding the most intelligent way to implement plans. Not only do they enjoy this, but they expect potential partners to enjoy this process also. They prefer that this exploration of ideas and exchange of strategies occur in the most harmonious manner possible, so that the discussions are simultaneously enriching and beneficial to the deeper level of interaction, which, for the Chinese, is the relationship itself.

They like all negotiations to feel as if valuable ideas and strategic skills are being shared between business friends. They appreciate dialogues that build bonds; wrap discussions in respect; give equal weight to all views; are unhurried and which enrich the bonds of relationship and the crucial issues of face and reputation.

Negotiation is also, for the Chinese, a continuation of the due diligence on character that they invest in greatly as a way of discerning the merits of future enterprise partners. The Chinese use negotiations to observe how we go after what we want; how we handle perspectives that are different from our own and the way in which we handle the inevitable twists and turns, peaks and troughs of the negotiating process.

They observe closely, during negotiations, to see if we do, indeed, share their approach to the negotiation itself. They further consider whether we are able, under the pressure of negotiating and driven by objectives and stakeholders, to retain and preserve the relationship strength as our primary business objective.

For Westerners, used to using negotiating as a robust debate and forthright setting out of terms, this feels like a very restrictive and limiting take on what negotiation itself means. However, if we cannot understand the implications of negotiating with our different semantic and cultural fields, how can we negotiate effectively in a way that produces success? Harmonizing our different approaches to negotiation becomes a very central and crucial skill set if we are to succeed in effective negotiation with the Chinese business culture.

In China, this can be simplified as follows: make the relationship more important than the negotiating process and the negotiations will be successful. This sounds like a bold premise and a rather risky strategy to Western business ears. It is not! In a relationship-centric culture, establishing publicly that both partners are equally invested in, and loyal to, the health of the business relationship allows it to flourish. The health of the business relationship, in turn, facilitates the ensuing negotiating process. Once both parties have signaled their commitment to relationships, the approach, tone, and manner, as well as the modus operandi of the negotiation itself, changes.

The tone, from the very beginning of the negotiation, will be softer, more respectful, consensus-seeking, and conciliatory; it will avoid harsh edges and the overly direct formulation of ideas. The manner of delivery will be more face conscious and more aware of how the message is received. As a result, the tone will be more solicitous of presenting the message in a way that is both accessible and acceptable to the receiver. This skill, which in intercultural communication is called metacognition (Chua 2012), will be at a premium, not just in our China dealings, but in all global exchanges and cross-cultural enterprise in the 21st century.

Metacognition is quite simply the skill of recognizing that everything we say has first gone through a culture, business culture, and personal

filter before being received by the person we are addressing. Ask someone from China, the United States, and France what the word *breakfast*
signifies and a series of cultural filters will produce different images of the
content of the meal itself and of when, where, how, and in what circumstances, it is eaten.

Imagine the implications when the word in question is no longer
*breakfast* but negotiation, partnership, accountability, or even consensus.
So, metacognition is understanding the cultural field of the person with
whom you are dialoguing and the cultural climate of those with whom
you seek to bond, trade, do business, and partner. Empathy is then added
to this understanding of the other's cultural preferences, understandings,
mindset, and values. The result is that when you present your ideas, goals,
and aspirations, you do so in a way that enables them to be well-received
and appreciated.

It is a wonderful skill for China since, by paying attention to the cultural reference points of your listener, you are showing supreme respect
for the business relationship, while simultaneously facilitating an optimum climate for negotiating consensus and successful outcomes. This is
yet another example of how using the tool of "relationship first" can sim-
plify negotiations with a culture who are often referred to in this context
as master strategists with an inscrutable style.

It may be tempting to use ruse, robustness, less than transparent strategy, or hard bargaining, but the truth is that the Chinese are expert in
these strategies and will quickly see through them. Their conclusion in
such instances is not, as it would be in the West, that you are a tough,
no-nonsense businessperson who drives a hard bargain, and who is not
above game playing to reach your objectives at all costs. Rather, the
Chinese will conclude that you are not serious about partnering with
them or succeeding alongside them since you are prepared to sacrifice
relationship to personal advantage.

In a person-centric business culture, where reputation is pure business
collateral, this means that you are a potential liability, an unsteady reputation partner, an unpredictable collaborator, and a partner who is likely to
create "poor face." Once the Chinese have decided this, negotiations no
longer have any chance of succeeding. They will stall, become prolonged,
or quite simply will be allowed to wither because the face-saving Chinese

will not wish to give a direct or definitive "no," even when they are sure that they no longer wish to proceed with you.

Once again, here is an illustration of the extent to which relationships drive success and facilitate all successful negotiation in China's business culture. Having provided the cultural context for negotiation in China, I will now show you, in detail, how deploying metacognition and cultural sensitivity, alongside your own negotiating prowess and skills, can work to great advantage for all your business goals and aspirations in China.

## Optimum China-Adapted Negotiating Styles

To become a successful negotiator in China, we must first embrace the understandings shared previously of what negotiation means to the Chinese, as both a concept and practice. We must further be mindful, at all times, of the contrasts that exist between Chinese and Western negotiating protocols.

Significantly, there is no single word for "negotiating" in Mandarin. Instead, it is translated by a composite of two characters 谈判 *tán*, which means discussion, and *pàn*, which means making judgment (Chen 2001). As expert commentators such as Ming Jer Chen (2001) point out compellingly, the emphasis falls upon the former of these characters, "tan," meaning discussion, for this is the core meaning in China of negotiation: an ongoing debate that seeks to secure positive and attractive outcomes harmoniously for all concerned. The Chinese enjoy negotiation because they view it in this way. They expect goodwill to be present at all stages. They do not engage in combative approaches and expect the negotiating process to be conducted not as a robust debate but rather as a respectful sharing of ideas, which is always mindful of group face and harmony.

For the Chinese, a hotly debated outcome that has caused upset to group dynamics is not considered a win. Similarly, an outcome that has taken face from the negotiating parties and which is perhaps only grudgingly accepted by some of the participating parties is considered a failure. The reason being that this process has violated the key facilitator for business exchange and for protecting deals: relationship health and harmony.

So, the Chinese approach negotiation with a composite goal: not solely to make a deal, but to make a deal which preserves harmony and face—a much more holistic objective. The holistic nature of the objective, in turn, changes negotiating tactics, style, content, and delivery. Let us look at this in more depth.

The Chinese like relaxed early-stage negotiation. In the same vein as the character due diligence, the Chinese favor an extended period in which to become acquainted and share ideas; this acts as a preamble to a fuller or more advanced negotiation. While China will expect both parties to deploy strategic negotiating prowess, they are more willing, and often more able to take extended periods of relationship building to establish the gravitas and parameters of a negotiation. The bonds created by such an approach act as a way of adding warmth and commitment to the early negotiation stages, by assisting the development of shared objectives in the initial phases of the negotiating process.

The significance of everything in Chinese negotiations is relational. The opening and final phases, which are warm and personal, as well as highly face-promoting and respectful, are held in the presence of senior company leaders and board members. The middle phases, which are crunchier and have greater potential for heated exchange or debate as well as the drilling down of finer points, are handled away from the senior company directors by seasoned negotiators from the China side who are carefully briefed, mandated, and given specific degrees of latitude in the negotiation.

All of this stems from Chinese attitudes to what business deals are. We, in the West, see them as finite transactions, a goal in themselves. For the Chinese, the deal is merely a marker within the much more important evolution of the business relationship. A deal can be undone. It is considered subordinate to the relationship. It is considered soft and must follow the natural organic shifts that any relationship would. In China, even when contracts are signed, there are many iterations, affirmations, and commitments needed before the safety of the contract is guaranteed in a way that we would recognize.

All of this can make us extremely nervous. For Western business culture, negotiation is a robust debate and the outcome, a hard-fought battle. We then expect to codify and ratify such outcomes with the help of contractual law; this, in turn, makes us feel secure in the knowledge that the deal is well underpinned. This is the case, whether or not the business relationship remains in its most harmonious, robust, or healthy condition, after such negotiations.

The parties proceed to implement what has been agreed because the contract obliges them to do so, with the threat of litigation to enforce terms acting as a powerful deterrent to breaches of contract. This is how we, in the West, define good faith. A functional business relationship, for us, is one where both parties adhere to the fixed terms of the contract, for the duration of its specified timelines. For the Chinese, this feels like a bad faith arrangement. If we do not trust the relationship we have built and the mutual benefit we seek to create, how can a piece of paper counteract what, to the Chinese, feels like a flawed and unsustainable partnership infrastructure?

Therefore, being a deft and capable negotiator in China comes back, yet again, to being sensitive to all aspects of the relational framework in which negotiations occur.

The first step is to acknowledge that negotiations take place within a strict company and social hierarchy. Senior company directors in China expect to participate in phases one and three, with people of equal status and seniority. Similarly, a Chinese negotiating team will be given substantial power as well as a roomy mandate for negotiation. They will expect the Western negotiation team to have the same power, as they forge the details of this important negotiation. The Chinese team will then be expected, given the vertical hierarchy in Chinese business, to take any prospective negotiation outcomes to their company leaders for scrutiny and refinement.

In China, negotiation is, above all, a matter of respect, face, and reputation both internally and between all parties concerned. It is crucial to emphasize status and underline commitment to win/win objective framing, as these elements are fundamental to the process of a successful negotiation in China. Begin, therefore, by carefully considering the matching of those participating in the negotiation from the perspective of status, hierarchy, and influence. This demonstrates how greatly you respect both the negotiation process and the status of your interlocutors.

Remember to empower your negotiating team and to give them public status; let your company director show attentiveness and respect, in person, within stages one and three, even if this can only occur by remote link. Find a way for the most senior people in the company to show their faith in those who will be working out the detail of the negotiation. This enables them to participate with a degree of authority; the same degree of authority as will be accorded the Chinese team by their leaders.

Keep the negotiations personal; let them feel loose and organic at every stage of unfolding. Refuse imperatives of deadlines, performance, and stakeholder impatience; these sabotage more Western negotiations than any other factor in China, often resulting in a snatching of failure from the jaws of success. Keep communication friendly, personal, and measured. Be willing to adhere to the general spirit of the deal, initially, rather than forcing specifics at too early a stage. Keep reading the room and taking the temperature of the relationship as, if this is right, the deal will evolve and will be one which satisfies all parties.

It is crucial never to score negotiating points at the expense of your prospective Chinese partners' reputation and face. If positions need to shift, frame any invitation to do so in a way that protects the face of all involved in the negotiation. Remember that relationships make deals in China, never the reverse.

Do everything you can to demonstrate and promote trust. The Chinese do the best deals with those they trust the most. In a business world governed by face and reputation, fostering and promoting trust is the most pragmatic of strategies and skills sets. Remember to take account of both cognitive and affective elements of trust, for the Chinese always do this.

By all means, demonstrate prowess and skill in negotiating but, alongside that, demonstrate character and show consideration and desire for consensus building; in negotiation, this may involve, at times, ceding ground in favor of collective harmony. This ground can later be regained through the strong relationship you have made and your overarching commitment to mutual benefit.

Often, it is helpful to make early concessions and reserve your core nonnegotiables for some of the last-minute deal brokering, which is common in Chinese business exchange. It is important to emulate the strengths of Chinese negotiators themselves and play well to these: be indirect, never confrontational; concede small points to empower later gains through the continuous building of a positive relationship; be modest in your assertions; frame your demands as benefits; demonstrate the face-giving elements of your deal; share knowledge; show the benefits to the wider community and culture, of the deal you are brokering.

Negotiations are prolonged in China and require commitment of time, energy, and frequency of visits. Shareholder and stakeholders are used to Western negotiation timelines. They must therefore be prepared for the extended timelines typical of Chinese negotiations. It is crucial that stakeholder expectations are managed so they do not become a pressure on the negotiation process. Without this, the pressure of our Western performance and outcome criteria makes us engage in missteps, often resulting in the loss of hard-won ground and opportunities.

Remember that of all the elements of advice given in his chapter, the most important is to put relationship at core of all you say and all you communicate. If you are sincere in this, an energy of win/win and implicit commitment to mutual benefit will emanate from your entire negotiating stance.

Nothing helps to engage the Chinese like trust and when this is effectively and sincerely communicated, all negotiations succeed. Once trust is fully established, progress often occurs at a rapid pace, with all the pieces falling into place in the most desirable form for all parties. Playing our part well in this, by understanding Chinese preferences in the negotiating process, is metacognition deployed in the service of our business skills and desired outcomes.

We can deploy cultural adaptation astutely to ensure that we are negotiating for success in the short term and longevity of association, in the longer term; doing so promotes cooperation and ensures optimum results for all concerned. The Chinese revere such an approach, above all else, in their Western partners; this is even more true, since it has become, in recent years, increasingly rare. When they identify this attitude in prospective Western partners, they are at once engaged and disarmed; suspicion lessens, leaving ample room to build a meaningful relationship; establish integrity of character, and create a forum for the most successful and enduring partnerships. This is the supreme negotiating stance; it is this which, when sincerely accomplished, ensures that negotiations will end not just in successful outcomes, but in the protection of the critical relationships that underpin these outcomes.

# CHAPTER 4

# Making Deals That Work and Last in China

### Deal-Making: Contrasting East/West Cultural Perspectives

The Chinese do not like short-term approaches to either business or life. Culturally, they are trained from infancy to believe that one must embrace a perspective that involves both the medium and long term, if wisdom is to be acquired and success is to be achieved. It is for this reason that we find contemporary business in China turning to, and being guided by, the revered wisdom of thinkers who lived millennia ago. These thinkers offer, to the Chinese mind, tried and tested advice that promotes long-term thinking.

This thinking is now a fundamental part of Chinese business culture and of the Chinese psyche. Given this preference for long-term thinking, the Chinese take extended lengths of time to consider and commit to business propositions and partners. They believe that, in doing so, they are more able to consider the impact of all decisions in the short, medium, and long term.

Since the Chinese remain intensely committed to the relationships they form, they like to display loyalty by resisting any unnecessary change or risk. They consider that such risks may alter the cherished status quo in their business relationships. Such an approach sits extremely well with being averse to short-term thinking. This makes the Chinese invaluable partners because alongside their loyalty, they also demonstrate full and robust engagement with the goals of their business partners, ensuring lasting success.

Their desire for mutual benefit and shared reputation encourages the Chinese to achieve success for their partners at all costs, because failure in such instances would harm both reputation and face.

Making the right deal for China means making a deal that works in the short term and endures into the future. This means ensuring that the deal is solid enough to stand the test of time. In the West, we do this through complex projection and prediction tools developed by business thought leaders in management science and governance. In contrast, the Chinese do this by underpinning the business process with a strong relationship and a robust set of business bonds. Such bonds are capable of weathering any contingency or adversity, thereby effectively future-proofing any deal made.

To participate in this incredibly supportive and lucrative deal model, we must show that we hold the same cultural values around deal-making. We must demonstrate that it is the deal we make that serves the relationship and not the relationship that serves the deal. This latter formula is more typically what we aim for and experience in Western business deal-making. We must show that we have come not just to "play" but to "stay."

China, like the West, wants security around its deals. Security in a reputation-centric culture, however, involves making wise choices of partners, high levels of joint engagement, and shared public face. Avoiding short termism, opportunism, or quick profits, which are seen as the enemies of this cherished security, plays well to Chinese sensibilities. This is because the Chinese prefer ethical business partnerships and processes, which they can be proud of publicly, and not just celebrate on a profit statement.

This concern for reputation and security makes the Chinese willing to share only if there is clear evidence from us of a "here to stay, not just to play" approach from us. This approach must apply to any and all deals we seek to make with them. Once again, for the Chinese, this is a way of flushing out the true nature of our character and business ideology. If they see undue haste, a desire for quick market dominance, overly robust initial price points and a "profits only" focus, they recoil!

This is because, once again, these tactics are at odds with China's slow, steady, organic business ideology that has one eye on the present, medium, and long term and one eye on relationship health and reputation.

Reputation facilitates deals while relationships underpin deals. Empathy, along with good people-handling skills, ensure that success is long-lasting. Such success must always be achieved without ever harming the precious business collateral that is public reputation in this face-dominated business culture. How a deal is done matters; how a deal is protected matters; how a deal is made to have longevity matters even more. In China, relationship, face, and reputation are the modus operandi for securing deals, wrapping optimum reputation around them, and creating precious longevity.

We will look now in detail at some helpful strategies for making truly great deals and ensuring that any hard-won enterprise success that you achieve endures.

## Developing Successful Deals With China

The deal in China, as with all other business goals, must be seen in the context of the relationship-centric culture in which it is set. Thus, it must be about a shared objective that creates, in equal measure: face, reputation, and mutual benefit for all parties concerned. It must, further, be the outcome of the harmonious sharing of knowledge, wisdom, and ideas in a common business pursuit or objective.

If this feels lofty to our more pragmatic and transactional Western business sensibilities, it, in no way, appears idealistic or abstract within the Chinese business culture paradigm. It is instead the perfect intersection of concerns for progress (deal, contract, transaction) and concerns for partnership (relationship, face, and reputation); this intersection, in turn, is this space where all success happens in China.

When do we know that we have fully grasped the primordial importance of relationships in China? When we have understood that developing partnerships and signaling our trustworthiness to undertake relationships must always be reflected in our ability to frame deals, in ways that benefit all parties. By doing this, we show how committed we are to harmoniously conducting and concluding the deal in question.

There is no room in this model for the kind of ruthless, hard bargaining, which is exclusively deal and advantage-oriented but which neglects the health of the business relationship. To avoid this, we must ask ourselves how we can frame and close deals in a way that does not compromise crucial relationships. Deals cannot be achieved either through rushed interactions or an exclusive focus on deal-making success and forced outcomes.

We do this, first, by embracing the core understanding that relationship success is the major facilitator and true protector of all deals made with China. We must embrace this fully whether it is an inconvenient truth for us, or not. We must embrace this fully whether it suits our more transactional business operating methods, or not. We must embrace this fully whether it is our preferred way to deploy skills in the deal-making process, or not. We must do this because we know it to be a fundamental truth in Chinese business culture that deals only happen because of relationships and that failure to successfully nurture relationships breaks deals irrevocably. We must do this because we now know that the reality of China business is that when relationships are neglected or falter, deals will either end up stalling indefinitely or imploding.

So, embracing this truth is the number one strategy both for launching deals and succeeding in closing and protecting them. When we have accepted the primacy of relationship in terms of deals, it will create in us a disposition that sends different and very welcome signals to the Chinese. This signals that the deal we are here to discuss must be done, from our perspective, with huge attention to the health of the business relationships underpinning the deal and must be carried out with the firm objective of mutual benefit.

Since our attitudes and responses tend to follow our core values, this new disposition will encourage us to ensure that our responses and attitudes stay relationship-friendly, as we progress the deal. Equally important, it will help us frame the deal in ways which show the Chinese that we have come to participate in a China-adapted deal journey. The Chinese greatly appreciate this business attitude. In China, the deal is very much a journey, rather than a destination ratified by law and underpinned by processes, as in the West.

If we adopt the below strategies, we will signal a real will to partner and make lasting deals, in ways which appeal to the Chinese and their deal-making sensibilities.

Aim, where possible, to:

- Present the deal in ways that show your commitment to
  your partners, their organization, leadership, business goals,

relationships with their city, their stakeholders and their government partners (as the latter often sit on corporate boards), as well as their wider reputation, public face, and community standing;

- Frame the deal discussions in ways that show your commitment to partnership and harmony, as this signals that you will never sacrifice these core values for quick wins and outcomes; this, in turn, encourages the Chinese to view you as a worthy and safe reputation partner;
- Work hard to increase trust levels, as you establish the parameters of the deal;
- Show your commitment to both cognitive and affective trust-building to accompany the evolving stages of the deal; do this by sharing knowledge to build effective trust; remember that knowledge sharing acts as a conduit for business bonding and trust-building in China;
- Go above and beyond what is needed—this establishes a Chinese-style commitment to partnership;
- Provide ways to share and enrich competencies and capabilities as the deal progresses;
- Be willing to go slowly and demonstrate a patient disposition, as this is viewed as a mature business skill in China and elicits great respect;
- Allow the deal to progress as the relationship matures, at a pace that echoes the rhythm of the unfolding relationship;
- Ensure that it is the relationship that determines the evolution of the deal rather than the reverse;
- Avoid searching uniquely for outcomes or wins;
- Always be willing to reassess or reframe objectives, to preserve the health of the relationships, since the latter facilitates outcomes;
- Always keep faith in progress even if it appears slow;
- Remember that a great deal happens behind the scenes in China and conclusions can be refreshingly sudden and satisfactory;
- Manage stakeholder pressure; this is something the Chinese do brilliantly;

- Always stay in sync with the rhythm of patient progress rather than forcing the deal-making pace;
- Constantly monitor for any breaks in the relationship flow; remember that such breaks show up, typically, as awkward silences, procrastination or delays;
- Step back from the deal discussions, if you observe the relationship waning, and focus all your energy and commitment on rebuilding the relationship;
- Avoid undue emphasis on profit seeking or displaying harsh deal-making techniques;
- Avoid overtly cunning tactics as these feel manipulative to the Chinese and risk harming the relationship;
- Communicate ethics in all your deal discussions as this promotes transparency and greater accountability in your Chinese partner;
- Remember that trust protects against duplicity;
- Look for as many ways as possible to build trust and to give trust, model trust, and foster trust throughout the whole deal-making process.

All the aforementioned, signal to China that your attitudes and disposition, with respect to deals, sit safely and harmoniously with theirs. Another fundamental consideration is how you treat your Chinese interlocutor during the process of deal discussion and deal-making itself.

To ensure the smooth passage of your deal, ask yourself the following questions:

- Is the deal discussion being conducted respectfully?
- Is everyone able to define the parameters equally and equitably?
- Is the negotiation space equally shared?
- Is the manner of conducting the discussion such that it will enhance the face and status of all participants?

These would feel like secondary and very superfluous concerns to Western businesspeople who expect robust, concise, and effective exchanges of deal-making tactics, leading to a speedy and profitable conclusion. At that point, potentially, the relationship itself may strengthen and flourish, as a result of a deal well done. This is not, however, the optimum template for progressing deals that work for the Chinese.

For an earlier book, I had the privilege of setting up interviews with a number of Chinese CEOs across diverse fields such as manufacturing, plastics, education, and pharmaceuticals in northeast China (Turley 2010). I asked for their views on key topics such as deal-making, partnership, project management, and governance. In the course of these interviews, the Chinese CEOs complained that the peremptory, overly robust, and often hasty way in which Western counterparts progress deal discussions, signals a disinterest in the relationship itself. It further suggested to the Chinese CEOs an exclusive interest among Western CEOs on profits and "winning."

Conducting deals in this manner makes the Chinese feel devalued. It also takes away their face and it makes them suspicious of businesspeople who appear to believe that such behavior could be conducive to the creation of a profitable deal or lasting partnership.

It is quite easy to see, from a relational business culture perspective, why such conduct would harm deal potential and compromise business partnerships and cooperative trade. The fact is that when the Chinese have decided that you are a worthy partner in face and reputation and have evaluated the deal or project as worthy, they will automatically seek to create mutual benefit. Moreover, they will see it as an obligation to ensure the success of the deal discussions. It becomes for them a matter of pride and reputation to do so.

If, as your deal or partnership discussions progress, this appears not to be the case, you must ask if the relationship has been successfully made or if you do, indeed, have the right partner. The Chinese are tough negotiators. However, if they value the relationship, they will make sure that you reach your objectives, provided that you pay attention to protecting their face, and are fair in what you are willing to concede within the deal discussions.

The concepts of holistic integration and win/win or mutual benefit are deeply engrained in China's values set and social/business dynamics (Chen 2001). This is why it is so crucial for the Chinese that both parties feel respected and satisfied in terms of outcomes achieved. Given that the ultimate goal, for the Chinese, is partnership and longevity of association;

they are generally risk- and change-averse. They are intensely loyal and expect all business partners to avoid taking risks for short-term gain, however significant, since this would potentially sabotage the health of the business relationship. To do this, the Chinese would say, is neither pragmatic nor sustainable in a world where reputation is success collateral.

It is also crucial in understanding the Chinese to know that that they do not fear setbacks but regard them, rather, as opportunities. Moreover, since it is believed that good relationships will always be carriers of progress and positive outcomes, setbacks in deals are not to be feared. If a deal does not as progress as hoped, then the investment in the relationship will eventually produce a different, but equally positive, version of the deal. It helps that the Chinese attitude of patient progress and the core Chinese belief in *wēijī* (危机)—opportunity and crisis being two faces of the same phenomenon—enables them to take the long view, secure in the knowledge that through the medium of firmly established business relationships, the right deal will eventually be made.

To cope well with this approach, as Westerners who hold different attitudes to time and pace in the business context, we need to shift our emphasis and where we place our trust. We need to move away from constant, interim markers of success and quick deal fixes. We need to embrace the belief that nurturing the relationships behind the deal, as well as adopting an attitude of patient progress, will facilitate the progress of the deal, not slow it down.

We need to further accept that building relationships through cultural accommodation and bonding, strengthening our relationship rapport, showing good character, and professing a dedication to mutual benefit will produce the desired outcomes for us and for our business endeavors.

All of this presupposes that you have chosen well in terms of potential partners and that you understand the rules of good faith engagement. In China, it is both advisable and much easier, to flush out less than perfect partners, early in the deal-making process, if you apply the same relationship and characters litmus tests that the Chinese themselves do.

If you have, indeed, identified that a partner is not the correct one for you, you will find it easier to move to your next potential partner if you handle this situation sensitively and with no loss of face to others. Handling the situation in this manner will ensure that new potential partners, often of a higher caliber, will speedily emerge.

Most of all, it is important to feel both secure and grounded in the belief that the cultural adaptation of your business skills can, and will, promote trust and relationship harmony. Learn to see these skills for what they are: the most pragmatic and effective of business guarantors and dealmakers in a business culture where, ultimately, the relationship *is* the deal!

# CHAPTER 5

# Protect the Relationship to Protect the Deal

## Protecting Deals and Relationships: Contrasting East/West Perspectives

A huge part of protecting deals in China lies in our relationship with law and its relationship, in turn, with deals. Assuming we have used all the correct strategies to create excellent business relationships and underpinned all deals with genuinely strong and resilient business bonds, we will have gone much of the way to creating the enterprise success we desire. This presupposes, of course, that have nurtured these bonds and shown commitment to potential partners in the short, medium, and long term.

How do we then go about securing and sealing the deal? On a semantic/word association basis, "sealing the deal" or "securing the trade" to many Western businesspeople would mean tough legal negotiations, a watertight contract with strong terms of engagement and astute, and if necessary combative, lawyers.

Law, we believe in the West, protects by first defining, then ratifying, then enshrining in unbreakable terms, the essence of the deal. Law is not a celebration, more of a protector, a security giver, and an impediment to contract departures; it is how we manage the longer-term health of the deal by providing a framework of how we "must" now operate and how we should, going forward, conduct our business relationship.

Law used this way, however, becomes the invisible third leg of what was, in Chinese terms, a precious relationship based on character, shared objectives, and win/win outcomes. The Chinese are excessively wary of giving so much power, as an organic relationship culture, to something as codified and often adversarial as business or contract law. For them, the relationship that has carried the deal will sustain the deal, if we treat it with respect and underpin it with proofs of good faith.

The Chinese do, of course, acknowledge the role of business law but see it as a tool for the relationship, to hold the parameters of agreement, and as a written celebration of the bonds built. On the other hand, they do not see it as a stick to be wielded or a way of fusing unhappy, mismatched, or less than committed business partners or goals. Lawyers in China, adept at operating in a relationship-centric business environment, weave law around the relationship, never the reverse. The Chinese will expect our lawyers to possess the requisite skills to dialogue with theirs and operate in a similar fashion. Nowhere is this more to the fore than in the area of Intellectual Property Rights (IPR).

When I researched this area with a prominent Chinese IPR lawyer, I was astonished to discover a critical fact: one that is rarely communicated to Western businesspeople (Turley 2010). What the evidence demonstrated was that where the health of the business relationship was strong, intellectual property infringement was much rarer, more modest, and more easily repaired (ibid.). In recent years, China's willingness to heavily sanction infringements has provided further proof that relationship and reputation matter supremely to China. It further demonstrates that the Chinese care deeply about perception, even in the sensitive areas of legal rights and ownership of knowledge.

By understanding the Chinese cultural context for law, knowledge ownership, and deal protection, we can begin to signal, through our choice of lawyer and our attitudes to legal ratification, that our primary and enduring commitment is to the relationship. By doing so, we will further demonstrate that we can participate fully, astutely, and equally in a business model where protecting the relationship is tantamount to protecting the deal.

## Keeping Deals Safe

Deals, knowledge, and the avoidance of conflict in China all rely heavily on cultural understandings, business culture protocols, culturally adapted attitudes, and culturally aware investment in relationship handling. Many of these insights, protocols, and understandings differ from those dictated by our Western business culture. In China, these are largely framed around maintaining the optimum health of our business relationships. In the West, these would be heavily dictated by success, efficiency, and the rate of progress we achieve in reaching outcomes.

Once again, we find that in these key areas of business success with China the overarching task is a relational one. The advice, around protecting deals is, therefore, also anchored in the management of relationship, attitudes, and behavior. Let us look at three key business priorities, in the context of China, for protecting deals.

Western business negotiations tend to see the deal as the goal—an end in itself—and, therefore, the most important thing to achieve and protect. Once a deal is done, we tend to seal our gains through law. We leave the lawyers, who are the ultimate low context negotiators, to secure a robust contract and a framing of outcomes that protects our interest. In many ways, the "honeymoon period" is over with the signing of the deal. Thereafter, we rely on law, with its framework of accountability and threat of sanctions, to keep the parties in check throughout the implementation phases of the deal.

Such a model does not protect the deal in Chinese business understanding without having first protected the health of the business relationship, which underpins the deal. Indeed, it is the antithesis of a proof of good faith and most certainly does not signify, for the Chinese, either true protection or the long-term cementing of gains.

Law is a small part of how the Chinese ratify a deal; it is merely one composite element of the process. Moreover, how we choose to deploy legal structures and how they are applied in China is of paramount importance and can either seal or undo a deal. So, how do we protect deals in China and when should we begin to introduce law into the mix?

First, we must ensure that the passage to the deal has been smooth. We must have preserved face and China's hierarchical business style in the matching of our negotiators' status. We must have displayed attentiveness to public reputation and ideally avoided displays of ego, heated arguments, and any hint of "winner takes all" opportunism. We must have shown an appetite for patient progress and signaled, in everything we have done throughout the negotiations, that we have fully embraced

the core tenet of Chinese business culture: that social dynamics and relationship building is the fundamental aspect of strategy to be respected
and nurtured in business.

Part of this concern for relationship involves finding ways to blend
key elements of Chinese and Western approaches to trade and partnership implementation. It is important to integrate Chinese approaches to
accountability, project management, the choosing and management of
teams, and the handling of timelines for both delivery and achievement
of profit level. To protect all our key business relationships, it is important
to factor in that the Chinese consider short-, medium- and long-term
perspectives. Therefore, it is crucial to be thorough, cooperative, com-
prehensive, and willing to explore all these key areas as you negotiate the
deal, at the outset. By doing this, you avoid placing stress on or harming
the relationship in the medium and long term. It is also important, for
example, to understand that the Chinese approach market entry with the
intention of first proving their worth to that market.

To facilitate successful market entry, the Chinese are willing to accept
low initial price points and to show extreme patience in terms of speed of
yield. Instead, they content themselves with a gradual elevation of price
point and a slower delivery of profits. For these reasons, it is common
in China to forego robust initial profits when negotiating and earning a
place in a market sector than we would like to see within Western models.
China will often advocate sustaining a low price point for a longer period
than Western companies who, having invested in what they see as a prolonged time period to negotiate and seal the deal, are usually keen to see
higher revenue generation from the early stages of market entry.

Differences in market positioning and reputation in the sector, as well
as in schedules for revenue generation, all need to be explored and further
explored until a mediated, culturally adapted approach is achieved. The
Chinese do not delegate such discussions to lawyers, nor do they leave it
to the stage of legal ratification, as they see such discussions as the very
stuff of partnership and not merely the fine print within the terms of
a contract.

They will also require extended discussions of the staffing and people
side of a deal. It is crucial to ensure: that all staff retain their jobs; that
accountability is collective and teamwide and that the management of

staff is empathetic, holistic, and committed. We need to do this alongside acknowledging the vertical hierarchy that prevails in China's status-led business culture. Remember that people matter above all else, and management is often paternal in the care and attention they show to those they manage.

Overt or undue pressure on delivery timelines, insisting on early profits, and putting the spotlight on individual accountability look, to China, like poor relationship management.

Time, in China, is seen as serving the relationship, rather than the reverse. Excessive rigidity, typical of our Western approach, in this area, is frowned upon in China as it elicits poor performance from the Chinese and harms key relationship bonds and strengths. To the Chinese, this looks unskilled as a management strategy and somewhat unenlightened as a governance style. Moreover, such a style has no place when one manages and leads a people-centric business climate, where face is of critical importance and where one must seek to create loyalty, harmony, and relationship health.

So, the implementation phase of the deal needs to be looked at cautiously and thoughtfully, with the prevailing disposition to accommodate our contrasting business cultures and to make compromises, where necessary. Protecting the deal, here, means using the space of a well-constructed relationship to thoroughly explore the short-, medium-, and longer-term aspects of staffing, project management, accountability, implementation, and delivery timelines, as well as profit schedules and projections. This valuable investment of time, energy, and commitment to managing the deal in ways that protect the relationship is your primary protector of the very same deal. This is particularly critical because, in China, what happens after the deal is as important as the deal itself, which is merely a marker, albeit a crucial one, in the evolution of a continuing business relationship.

In order, therefore, for the deal to be solid and to remain secure, it must be underpinned by strong relationship bonds and excellent communication. It further requires a continued and visible commitment to mediating contrasting approaches to the business process. This is how the deal stays safe in Chinese law. In a very real sense, the contract itself is viewed as cementing the deal done on the back of a strong relationship.

The contract functions and remains viable only if the relationship flourishes and remains intact. If the relationship deteriorates and cannot be repaired, the Chinese will find an exit route, even if this involves a financial loss. Successful relationships and harmony matter most to the Chinese; success in China simply cannot be sustained without attention to these factors.

China likes to issue significant markers of relationship progress in the form of Statements of Intent and through the popular, and respected, format of Memoranda of Understanding. However, they view these as celebrations of progress, rather than a codification of irrevocable terms. The more important security-giving functions of these documents is the opportunity they present to celebrate and codify the deal through the public face exercises, which accompany the exchange of these documents. Such ceremonies usually involve the photographing of both partners and the public creation of shared reputation. This is what truly seals the deal in China; these exercises in public face are the true markers that map out and protect our progress in the Chinese business culture.

## Law and the Protection of Knowledge in China

A key element of trust as it exists in China is the sharing of knowledge, expertise, competencies, and skills with those we wish to partner. Knowledge has been considered for many centuries in China as a universal value and this belief has, historically, deeply informed China's position on knowledge share and ownership. Despite being a world leader in registering patents for new products, services and innovations, China has been incredibly slow, given its cultural beliefs, to protect its own IPR.

Confucius, the most influential of Chinese thinkers, stated, "I transmit rather than I create" (Soetendorp 2008), thereby highlighting the belief that that knowledge belongs in the common and collective arena, benefiting all. It further emphasizes that the Chinese can view our Western desire for absolute territoriality of knowledge ownership as both avaricious and insensitive. When we display such territoriality over knowledge ownership to the Chinese, it looks very much like we do not trust them, nor the partnership we are seeking to build with them. This is what they deduce from our highly protective approach to intellectual property: that we wish, in fact, to hide our competencies and store of knowledge from them, rather than sharing what we know. All of this constitutes multiple affronts to face and is absolutely guaranteed to weaken the underlying relationship, which is, in fact, the true protector of knowledge in China. So how do we protect our own intellectual property, without damaging the relationship, giving proofs of bad faith or harming face?

First, by accepting this key overriding principle: my intellectual property is unlikely to be threatened, taken, or eroded if I choose my partner well. I can further protect this by establishing mutual benefit and joint face, and by taking care of the health of my business partnership at every juncture. This is the core point of departure and disposition which will protect your IP. Indeed, as I noted earlier, in the majority of cases where IPR have been threatened in China, the underlying relationship had weakened, mutual benefit had not been established, and the health of the partnership had been neglected (Turley 2010). Breaches of IPR in almost every case were traced back to ruptures in the relationship rather than emanating from IPR self-interest or opportunism exclusively.

It follows, therefore, that the best way to protect your intellectual property in China is to establish cognitive and affective trust within the partnership. This is further cemented by extending mutual benefit to the enrichment of partners' competencies and knowledge base. To the Chinese, when Westerners engage in this way, it constitutes the ultimate win/win. It acts as a proof of good faith and a commitment to the relationship itself. It engenders trust and suggests that we do, indeed, want our Chinese partners to thrive through and alongside us.

Given the historical belief within China that knowledge is, indeed, a universal value, any sharing of knowledge on behalf of Westerners is seen as particularly respectful and marks us out as especially worthy to trade and partner with the Chinese (Soetendorp 2008).

We should take heart also from the fact that given China's current awareness of the views we hold toward intellectual property protection, coupled with its desire to partner us, huge steps have been taken by China to make IPR more secure within their business culture.

As early as 2010, it was recorded that an impressive number of high-profile IPR infringement cases were being settled in favor of Western business companies (Turley 2010). This, alongside other IPR protection initiatives, has increased our confidence in China's willingness to protect our intellectual property and, indeed, to sanction any theft of Western intellectual property.

Progress in this area has been consistent and sustained in China (Soetendorp 2008). This ranges from partnering with Western firms to establish intellectual property academies, to training the next generation of corporate leaders and Chinese civil administrators, to creating major initiatives at the school, college, and university level explaining Western preferences and attitudes to intellectual property protection (ibid.).

In undertaking such initiatives, China is seeking to create a new and informed generation as well as a countrywide understanding of what needs to be done to make Western companies feel safe in this area. How, then, can we signal reciprocity in this field? Here are some strategies:

- Do not allow your protectiveness on IPR to appear greater than your dedication to the relationship.
- Remember the principle of mutual benefit: share knowledge, competencies, and skills where you can.
- Remember that building reciprocity and effective trust is a public face issue in China.
- Give Chinese counterparts assistance and share knowledge, where possible. This is always deeply appreciated and will be repaid elsewhere, as business assistance toward goals and success.
- When using law to ratify deals, choose lawyers with full cultural awareness of the Chinese emphasis on the primacy of relationships. Choose lawyers who remain relationship-focused and sensitive in their handling of IPR, as this signals to the Chinese that you value relationships above all else.
- Always remember that, assuming your partner due diligence has been thorough and you have chosen well: if relationships flourish, Intellectual Property Rights remain intact and knowledge share is reciprocal. So, while the learning curve may appear steep, and the character due diligence arduous, once these are achieved, precious IPR are truly protected and future proofed.

## Avoiding Conflict

As previously highlighted, relationships well-made and well-maintained are the greatest protectors of harmony, which is considered a primary goal and core value in Chinese business culture. In most instances where conflict occurs within business dealings with China, trust levels have typically come under significant strain, prior to the emergence of the conflict. Most frequently, this is because culturally maladapted behavior has resulted in poor attention to the relationship and the building of joint reputation.

The balancing of demands and gains, the maintenance of visible levels of reciprocity, and the creation of win/win outcomes and mutual benefit are all needed to preserve the face of every party involved and protect the relationship from deteriorating.

Deterioration does occur, however, when Western businesses, fearful of inadequate levels of progress and profit schedules, allow these factors to outweigh the need to preserve the relationship. It is challenging for us, at such moments of business pressure, to give the requisite levels of attention to face. It is also difficult, under the pressure of outcomes, to work toward reputation-protecting solutions to any challenges that arise in the areas of delivery, implementation, and profit creation.

Often the tone at such junctures, from Western businesses, becomes more robust, pressurizing, and outcome-directed. Instead of speeding up desired results, this harms relationships and causes disharmony. Even more significantly, it creates ruptures within the very partnerships that are the ultimate carriers and facilitators of progress and positive outcomes.

To avoid conflict, therefore, think face, reputation, and mutual benefit even at times of high stress. Make this more than an attitude or occasional reference point. Make this your disposition—one that is clearly on show and prevalent in all your behaviors, responses, discussions, and negotiations. Yield ground where you can, if it will have the effect of strengthening the relationship. This is the ultimate example of ceding small points to win huge rewards. In the content, tone, and register you adopt, think reputation and partnership. Make these your prevailing idiom and guide. Take extra care with witnessed discussions; the presence of third parties means that the discussion, within Chinese business culture, is now a matter of face and reputation and, therefore, must be handled with additional delicacy.

If you have difficult or challenging matters to discuss, do this privately, ensuring at all times that you offer a breadth of leeway in discussing potential options. Never corner a Chinese partner to win a point of negotiation or a competitive edge. Always be respectful to their broader obligations; respect their sector, company, city, and province as these form part of the wider reputation of the Chinese business partner you seek to court.

In terms of mindset, always think "we" not "I" since, in all your interactions, your partnership is your success in China. Believe in mutual benefit as a core business objective, not just an accessory. Let it guide you and steer you. Make a commitment to this as the core signaler of all your behavior and interactions. If your business values are rooted in this desire for mutual benefit, it will assist your behavior to be always China-adapted.

Above all, remember that the Chinese do not like to fail. Failure offends face and sabotages their obligation to preserve reputation in a person-centric society. If you build and preserve trust and partnership harmoniously, you will be included in the "no fail" rule of Chinese business. Within this template, if business problems cannot be solved directly, they will be solved using networks, relationships, and lateral or strategic means (Chua 2012). Either way, the Chinese will ensure that you are an integral part of the success and reputation created, provided that the health of these core business relationships always remain your overriding concern, objective, and preoccupation.

# CHAPTER 6

# Repairing and Rebuilding the Relationship

## Conflict Resolution, China Style

### Conflict Resolution: East/West Perspectives

Handling conflict resolution with China, successfully, requires an understanding of the dissimilar and sometimes opposing definitions held by China and the West of what conflict is. Typically, for Western businesses, conflict occurs when something has happened to threaten our goals, such as the stalling of a negotiation or the departure from the terms of a negotiated contract. In such cases, we react to the potential loss of negotiating collateral and business power. We, in the West, also engage in conflict when something has occurred to threaten our interests. An example of this could be a rupture in the progress of a deal or a challenge to expected profit schedules, shares, or ROI. Once again, in this instance, we are reacting to the potential loss of collateral—in this case financial—and engaging in conflict as a result of this threat. The West further tends to engage in conflict when something has occurred that threatens our intellectual property ownership, resulting, as we see it, in a potential loss of intellectual collateral if we do not use conflict to resolve the issue.

In China, conflict has significantly different roots and origins. Conflict arises when the negotiating styles or behavior of Western partners threatens the Chinese business partner's reputation (Turley 2010). In such cases, the pursuit of profit and negotiating advantage has become more important than relationship and reputation, which risks harming the public face and standing of the Chinese. Since reputation is key collateral in China, within the business and wider community, the Chinese feel drawn to conflict when this is compromised. Moreover, when the business behavior of a Western partner threatens Chinese guanxi networks and compromises the relationships, obligations, and responsibilities which every Chinese businessperson has, conflict often arises through the Chinese seeking to retrieve lost dignity and standing.

In China, dignity and mutual benefit go hand in hand, thereby signaling that the individual and his company understands their role, not just in the business culture, but within the wider social fabric of the collective, which is so dear to Chinese people. The Chinese feel compelled to adopt a strong stance when these cherished core values are contested or compromised.

The contrast is clear: we, in the West, enter into conflict when the processes that underpin our business progress, goals, and profits are threatened. Whereas China enters into conflict when its relationship collateral, which it sees as fundamental to business and to life, is threatened.

Once again, as explained in our earlier consideration of optimal negotiation and conflict avoidance strategies, we see that contrasting priorities and business emphasis are the demarcation lines around potential areas of conflict. For the West, this is about protecting our processes; for China, it is about protecting the relationships that underpin such processes.

It is, in essence, merely a matter of emphasis and by no means constitutes an insurmountable cultural or commercial distance. Yet, the potential for conflict, aborted deals, cultural misunderstandings, and sabotaged business relationships is huge. As an intercultural adviser and businessperson, it has been disappointing to observe gratuitous conflicts in business relationships sabotage viable partnerships, meaningful enterprise, and mutually enriching projects. This has often occurred simply because each party had retreated unilaterally into what they considered to be their individual priority and omitted to pay respect to the cherished priorities of the other party, organization, and culture. The first tenet of conflict repair is to acknowledge that, at the level of our priorities, a disconnect has occurred. We must then promptly display the will to stop such a disconnect becoming irretrievably deeper.

Assuming then, for the reasons stated above or other, conflict has arisen in our dealings with China, how do we successfully defuse it? The advice on conflict resolution that I am about to give falls broadly into two categories. First, what we should resist doing if conflict has arisen in our dealings with China and, second, what strategies and attitudes we must adopt if we are serious in our quest to repair these relationships compromised by conflict. Let us expand the context of this advice by examining, more fully, how conflict arises in our dealings with China.

## The Origins of Conflict

When business fails to progress in China, it is typically due to parity or reciprocity, fundamental concepts to the Chinese, becoming compromised or threatened. This occurs frequently when one commercial party engages in an overly one-sided and zealous pursuit of business objectives and goal. This is often combined with an inattention to the priorities and sensibilities of our Chinese partners, leaving them feeling that we operate on a profit-before-relationship basis, with our own unilateral interests having primacy over mutual benefit and shared reputation. While such imbalances lie at the heart of many conflict situations, they are significantly exacerbated when different cultural protocols and sensitivities are also in the frame.

We create conflict by allowing a disparity and lack of commonality to arise between us and our Chinese partners. This expresses itself at the level of priorities, vision, and differing paths to common goals. Often, the way in which we choose to define conflict reveals the nature of this problematic disparity, with all its potential for inducing discord. We, in the West, talk about the "going getting rough" when conflict occurs, whereas, in China, areas of challenge and conflict are framed in terms of the "relationship going bad." Bridging these definitions in moments when an atmosphere of conflict has arisen, and cultural sensitivities are rife, can be highly challenging. At such moments, we can unconsciously return to the norms of our own business culture for guidance. In the West, this often involves tough rhetoric and a strong, unyielding stance with an increasing emphasis on process to protect us. In China, it means retreating to protect one's network of broader relationships, which are, to the Chinese, sacrosanct. In both cases, from the perspective of the deal, project or business venture, everyone loses.

Typically, at such junctures, Western businesses will seek legal counsel; fine-tune the protections of IPR and minimize exposure. They will reiterate their negotiating stance with ever increasing robustness and finesse. Western businesses will further seek to look strong through reinforcing their position and strengthening negotiating boundaries until, to the Chinese, the latter appear more like walls. All of this is an attempt, on our behalf in the West, to feel secure and to retrieve ground when we feel that conflict has undermined our position.

The Chinese, conversely, will seek to protect the relationship and will insist on tangible proofs that the relationship does still, in fact, count, for the Western party. They will slow down all business processes and look for more, rather than less, from the Western party, not from a position of greed, but as proof of good faith. They will seek visible reassurance that the relationship behind the deal counts as much for us, as the deal itself. The Chinese will require more proofs of good faith as well as fresh acknowledgments on our part of the importance of reputation, public face, dignity, and guanxi networks. They will want us to show that we are, in fact, regretful of having harmed the above and, in so doing, harming the relationship. They will, above all, want warmth, sound character, strategies for relationship repair, and renewed commitment to mutual benefit and shared reputation to be highly visible from us.

Bridging these two approaches to conflict resolution is not easy. It is, however, possible, when we operate with intention and strong levels of intercultural awareness, to achieve this goal. Marrying these approaches is infinitely better than allowing the conflict to proliferate for, as any China advisor will tell you, this will always result in the loss of the deal and, more significantly, the loss of the relationship that underpins the deal.

## Recommitting to Priorities; Conflict Resolution Through Shared Vision

As stated above, conflict in an intercultural context often arises through conflicting priorities and disparities in the business approach that emanates from these. One of the first steps toward conflict resolution in our dealings with China is to find our way back to shared priorities. For the

Chinese, shared priorities are indicators of shared principles and, more importantly, of our values and character (Chen 2001).

For the Chinese, if priorities are not shared, then we cannot assume a set of shared principles, similar levels of goodwill, commitment to the business relationship, or to mutual benefit. Given that these are considered to be the fundamentals of good business partnership in China, the deal suffers if these values and attitudes are compromised. So, our first task in conflict resolution is to reharmonize our priorities. This often involves retrieving what has become lost in the business exchange which has led, in turn, to the conflict. In most cases of intercultural conflict that I have observed in China, and elsewhere, what had been significantly eroded or lost in the business relationship prior to conflict arising was *empathy*. In a relationship-centric business culture like China, empathy is a primary business skill. You will remember the skill of metacognition advocated earlier in this work. This is the skill of considering what we want and then putting this through the cultural filter and perspective of the person with whom we seek consensus, or rather, in this case, the person with whom we seek conflict resolution.

William Ury (2000), a brilliant and seasoned expert in negotiation and conflict resolution, talks about pausing in moments of conflict and "going to the balcony" to reconsider how priorities have become distanced or adversarial. By doing this, he suggests, we can begin to lay the bridge required for conflict resolution. Ury invites us to consider how the priority, goal, or method we are advocating could be presented by the other party to their stakeholders in a way that gains their approval. Engaging in this exercise often allows us to truly connect with the priorities of the other and take stock of the gulf that has arisen in our mutual priorities. It also encourages us to consider how methods and approaches that have given rise to conflict might not have done so had communication stayed strong and the relationship remained close.

Business expert Sir John Stuttard (2000) advocates being mindful of certain relationship and values-based criteria when trading with China. Inattention to these crucial values, in my own experience, can hinder successful trade, relationships, and conflict resolution. He iterated these central values and priorities as follows: flexibility, patience, *guanxi*, respect, and ethics (Stuttard 2000). These are the quintessential priorities for

China and the ones that make the Chinese feel incredibly secure and willing to trade and partner. The Chinese believe that if there is mutual commitment to these priorities, approaches, and business behavioral codes, then the processes so cherished by Western businesses can be accommodated. Moreover, and more importantly to the Chinese, such processes can be underpinned by solid business relationships, which act as powerful guardians of face and reputation as well as robust vehicles for success.

By revisiting the importance of relationships and by reframing our goals in terms of mutual benefit, we reach a shared vision that acts as a precursor to successful trade and partnership in China. We can also recommit to a methodology for achieving business goals that is patient, respectful, flexible, and ethically mindful of the business networks and reputational collateral of our Chinese business partners. To the Chinese mind, any recommitment to mutual benefit and relationship health as a primary priority removes the competitiveness and guardedness of transactional or adversarial business models. Such a recommitment creates a context of safety in which the Chinese can overcome challenges and resolve difficulties in a manner that is truly collaborative.

As stated earlier, in China, it is important to have not just a "win/win" where everyone gains but a "good win" in which the relationship, which is the lifeblood of all deals both future and current, can thrive and endure.

## From Reactive to Creative: Communication Strategies for Conflict Resolution

The expression "from reactive to creative" is part of an approach advocated by William Ury (2000) for handling moments of tension and conflict, both in dialogue and, more generally, in our trading relationships. Ury highlights how, in moments of conflict, certain cultures resort to unhelpful levels of reactivity, rather than focusing on self-mastery at such junctures and proceeding to creative solutions. This is particularly the case in cultures were emotion features prominently and is permissible in business dialogue. Reactivity and conflict flourish even more in business cultures, like ours, where robust expression is often seen as a business strength.

While this is an acceptable perspective and behavioral stance in Western business culture, this is by no means the case in China. Indeed, in Chinese culture, reactivity, and expressions of unchecked emotion in professional contexts, are discouraged. We are more likely to inflame situations and to fare less well in conflict resolution if we do not cultivate the ability to pause, or, as Ury likes to frame it, "go to the balcony." This counsel is particularly important in an intercultural setting where issues of not knowing how to "read" the other party heighten our sense of insecurity in moments of conflict and can make us doubly reactive and impulsive. By "going to the balcony" and reframing our own position in the light of fresh perspectives, which include the aspirations of our Chinese partner, we gain a valuable asset: the ability to make our communication nonreactive and free from harsh content and combative tones.

Moreover, we will be able to make the tone of our communication softer and more respectful once we have regained mastery of self and adopted fresh perspectives. Any seasoned commentator or advisor on China would affirm, categorically, that harsh words, robust speech, and combative approaches achieve nothing in this people-centric business culture. This is primarily because they harm face and, in so doing, negatively impact relationships.

In moments of conflict, it is important and crucial to adopt an even more measured, calm, soft, consensus-seeking mode of communication. Mandarin is a language built for consensus and reflects the fundamental desire of the Chinese to achieve outcomes based on mutual gain. In moments of conflict, we need to steer away from the many combative framings of business goals that exist in our more ruggedly individualistic Western business idiom and remember two things:

First, that Chinese culture intensely dislikes any form of disharmony. Second, that disharmony and disputes can be defused by adopting a communication style that is consensus-seeking. Such a style, when sincerely displayed, will always signal to the Chinese our genuine desire to return to harmony and well-being within the business relationship. When harmony is restored in the relationship, conflict lessens and with sustained attention to repairing the relationship through respectful communication, conflict will eventually evaporate.

## Reviving the Relationship: Conflict Resolution Through Respect and Entente

As stated previously in this work, conflict in business dialogue or within the interaction between parties can be traced directly back to ruptures in the relationship, whether these be overt or covert. A priori, repairing these relationship ruptures is the primary route to successful conflict resolution with China. Moreover, it is essential in relationship-centric cultures to acknowledge this fact. In the case of China, repairing the relationship is the primary recourse for conflict resolution rather than the resolute restating of absolute positions or recourse to law, which are increasingly the natural instincts of our Western business culture.

Successful conflict resolution with China begins with a wholehearted recommitment to the relationship as the primary priority and facilitator of all business goals and progress. Acknowledging the primacy of relationships will automatically soften our position. It will enable us to attack the problem while being soft on the people behind the problem (Fisher, Ury, and Patton 2011). It will also help us to reframe our approach to winning in a way that no longer fuels power conflicts. In the West, as Ury points out compellingly, winning makes us feel safe (2000). This is not the case in China. As Ming Jer Chen (2001), an enlightened voice on China points out, winning for the Chinese must always be a tie, since this promotes harmony and favors the continuing health of the relationship. When we understand that the fundamental desire of the Chinese in business situations is to arrive at a tie, we are less likely to pursue our attachment to winning, at the expense of the health of the business relationship.

Equally, we are less likely to have an immediate recourse to law in conflict situations—a behavior which the Chinese find intensely distasteful in their Western partners. The Chinese themselves are wary of early recourse to law in situations of tension or conflict, as they believe that it constitutes the ultimate sign of bad faith in the relationship (Chen 2001).

This is compellingly illustrated by Sir John Stuttard (2000), who argues convincingly that one of the most amicable settlements within the last decades of a large-scale dispute in China, was with McDonald's, who were asked to vacate their established Beijing site in 1994 by the Chinese government and city planners. By publicly framing their desire to respect and work with the objectives of the city planners and government, McDonald's were generously compensated, offered another site close by, and supported to open five other sites that year. Harsh words, judgments, and litigation would likely not have produced such a splendid result for McDonald's, nor ensured the continued thriving of their operations in China.

It is crucial to bring flexibility back in moments of conflict with China and equally crucial to frame our new flexibility in terms of respect, public face, and potential social benefit to our Chinese partners. This must also extend to their wider *guanxi* networks and communities.

Keeping disputes private and refocusing on the relationship is the very essence of good conflict resolution in China and always achieves results. China likes a win/win model to prevail everywhere in its business relationships. It further likes to proclaim harmony in family, work, and community relationships. It is the very core of the identity the Chinese wish to project. If the Chinese engage in conflict, it is because their dignity, face, and relationship collateral have been so publicly harmed or compromised that there is no other option than to retaliate. In so doing, they seek to preserve face and restore their dignity.

However, fundamentally, it goes against core Chinese values to engage in any form of public disharmony or conflict. Therefore, the moment that we signal a softer, more conciliatory approach, redolent of renewed commitment to relationships and shared vision, a desire will arise in the Chinese to join us wholeheartedly and gratefully. At such junctures, conflicts are immediately defused and challenges speedily resolved. In such moments, conflict resolution has occurred because we have taken the time to reiterate joint priorities, joint routes to our objectives, and joint benefits from outcomes achieved. This is what Sun Tzu, the author of the famous strategy manual *The Art of War*, meant when he talked about "winning without fighting" or the "bloodless coup" (McNeilly 2012). This is always the preferred route for the Chinese in terms of resolving difficulties and handling tensions in partnership as well as in the creation of trade and financial success. Nothing that is framed in adversarial terms succeeds in the Chinese business culture.

The Chinese believe that adversity builds strength and that this strength should always be deployed to create outcomes that holistically benefit all parties. Successful conflict resolution with China demands that we recommit to the principle of mutual benefit with great respect and in ways that preserve dignity. In such moments, the manner and tone of our communication matters enormously.

We, in the West, in moments of conflict, often lean heavily on a type of familiarity with our business counterparts to persuade them toward our point of view, perspective, and goals. It is crucial to remember that in communicating with the Chinese, familiarity does not signal respect. In fact, in moments of tension and conflict, the Chinese preference for asymmetrical deference, where formality is retained in addressing others, and a formal distance is maintained between the interlocutors, allows much more for the reestablishing of respect within our interactions. This is especially crucial since respect is the earliest casualty of conflict and the most essential value to reestablish within a people-centric culture of face and reputation, such as China. Formality of address is a staple of the asymmetric deference model allowing us, in moments of tension, the requisite distance for respect to be reestablished.

In their seminal work, scholars Scollon and Wong Scollon (2001) highlight that a first name-based appearance of business closeness makes Western businesspeople feel that they have gained relationship ground. For the Chinese, conversely, it often hampers the climate of respect needed, after the bruising experience of conflict, to help them feel safe once again.

Formal, deferential modes of communication and observing asymmetric deference at crucial points of conflict or tension shows that we are serious about conflict resolution and dedicated to manifesting respect for our Chinese partners. It further signals that we will take account, respectfully, of the values, preferences, and sensibilities of our Chinese partners in all our interactions with them.

Moreover, it demonstrates that we have the wisdom to make such factors more important than mere business advantage or a desire to maintain absolute business positions. It proclaims that we have reprioritized relationships, gained perspective, and recommitted to the primacy of respect and mutual benefit as the key vehicles for our joint goals and aspirations, as well as the ultimate carriers of their success. By doing this we are, in essence, telling the Chinese that we understand how to create and sustain a climate of safety in our relationships with them.

It is crucial, at this juncture, to remember that where there is safety, there will be no fear of loss to fuel potential conflict. On the contrary, where there is safety, harmony prevails, relationships thrive and enterprise flourishes.

# CHAPTER 7

# Creating and Maintaining Success With China

## Success Creation: Contrasting East/West Perspectives

Success, as defined within the Chinese business lexicon, whilst having many common features with our Western definition, also has its own unique properties. Understanding the deeply held view of success which the Chinese have, is central to adopting the right business attitudes for engaging in success-creation with this business culture. Firstly, success, like all other business definitions; commercial goals and values in China, must be understood in a relational context.

When the Chinese think success, they think relationship success, since relationships are the facilitators, arbiters and protectors of all positive outcomes. For the Chinese it is not just about the success we have, but the terms on which we have it. "Positive" outcomes which have been injurious to the health of core business relationships, would in no way be considered a real success in China. In such cases, business outcomes which harm relationships would be viewed as short term gain. Moreover, unless the relationship damage could be easily repaired, the cost of these gains would be considered by the Chinese to be overly high and unacceptable.

So, success for the Chinese is defined first and foremost in terms of relationships, both the nature of the bonds and their resilience. It is further defined as a combination of affective and cognitive trust on the part of the Chinese. Once achieved, this trust denotes that any business situation which the business relationship must face will succeed with optimum results and, significantly, with its reputational collateral intact.

How does all this tally with the definition of success which we are used to abiding by in the West? It is fair to say that there are, indeed, significant differences. We tend to think of monetary gain, market penetration, robust price points and early ROI as indicators that a successful trade, deal or partnership has been made. Whilst we like our business relationships to fare well and, ideally, flourish, we primarily require that they display competency, efficiency and professionalism. Above all, we expect our business relationships to have the ability to deliver expected results and projected profits. Beyond this, we do not share the concerns of the Chinese for the deeper health of the business relationship per se. Nor do we see this as an essential prerequisite or intrinsic requirement for achieving a measure of success with trade partners and others with whom we do business.

A healthy degree of joint competencies, shared standards of professionalism and a shared vision on projected targets, ROI and profit margins is usually considered more than ample. This is because we believe that contract law will do the rest, in terms of enshrining rights and responsibilities and sanctioning any departure from the latter.

So, we tend not to invest in the business relationship beyond the parameters of efficiency, joint professionalism, shared profits and a healthy ROI with, of course, some consideration for standards of governance and accountability. Our fundamental belief in the West is that it is the *process* of business which matters. We further believe that the health of this process and the smooth unfolding toward projected business aims, will allow the outcomes we need to flourish. It does not seem essential to us, therefore, to delve too far into relationship territory, the building of trust or the creation of strong bonds.

Beyond this, we rely on accountability, reporting, performance audits and checks and individual responsibility to carry us toward success and manage our trading relationships efficiently. This is usually accompanied by the willingness to replace or dismiss unsatisfactory team members or project managers with a view to protecting the health of the business process. All of this enables us to dispense with any sustained or intensive investment within the business relationship itself. We have replaced a relationship-centric focus with a process-centric focus and we believe that this is more than sufficient for success creation.

In China, where relationships matter phenomenally, accountability is teamwide, individuals are protected and any undue reliance on processes is viewed with a degree of caution. The Chinese believe that whilst business processes are important, they can also be unreliable, sterile and untrustworthy *if* they are not accompanied by loyalty to people and relationships. The Chinese prefer processes to be heavily supported by, and subservient to, the commitment between partners created by strong relationship bonds and public commitment to joint business philosophy, face and reputation.

It is the alliance of these two sets of values which makes the Chinese feel totally secure. Once the Chinese are secure and committed, they rarely fail to help the enterprises of their business partners to flourish. This is because in China, the success of a business partner is, fundamentally, your success, since the two are intertwined. Even greater than this, and of much more import to the Chinese, you have become an essential feature of their public face and reputation. Ensuring your success is a way of protecting their precious, and highly cherished, public face. In this model, if the Chinese allow you to fail, they fail. In sound relationships, where the Chinese have invested both the energy and resources to establish a robust and public joint profile, any failure on your part reflects on their capabilities. It also reflects on the soundness of judgment which they have displayed in choosing you as a partner, in the first instance.

To lose face would then be inevitable. This would, in turn, result in impoverished connections and compromised standing within Chinese business networks. Since these constitute the very pillars, facilitators and protectors of success they must never, within Chinese business philosophy, be impaired, compromised or harmed.

By understanding the primacy of concerns within the Chinese relational model, we can participate well and astutely within this model. Furthermore, we can show that we are both sincere and capable of understanding the model at depth. By displaying this depth of awareness and by applying the success strategies we will now recommend, you can ensure that your success is built in a sound, culturally adapted way; one which is solid and capable of achieving success with true longevity.

## Nurturing Success With China

Building trust and signaling respect in China begins with being well prepared and signaling competencies and talents which will enhance the reputation of your Chinese partners. The first rule in China is to come prepared to establish competency, mutual benefit and successful relationships. These play well to the affective and cognitive elements of trust-building which the Chinese value so deeply. By displaying what we have to offer in a polished, honed and reputation-enhancing way, we signal that we are ready to participate in character display and public face building.

China tends to be risk averse, and yet, matters of face prevent the kind of in-depth, direct and robust analysis which Western companies often subject each other to. Being willing to give proof of voluntary due diligence in terms of our character trustworthiness and business dealings, is a wonderful signaler of both respect and an informed understanding of the rules for building trust and partnership.

Ensure that your proposition is solicited in China and that there is, within your sector, the breadth to accommodate your presence as a new player. Look at how trading partnerships have been negotiated and legally supported, to date, in your field. Study the successes of Western companies who have gone before you. As you do this, common denominators will quickly emerge. Furthermore, you will quickly understand that that in most cases, their success was down, primarily, to their relationship building skills.

"Winning companies" in China will have invested heavily in spending time in China, from the earliest stages of the business dialogue, since they understand the necessity, in China, of doing business in person. Typically, successful Western companies will have grasped the face-to-face commitment required for building trust and partnership with this business culture. They will have chosen their most culturally-fluent and fluid executives to front their initiative. They will have ensured that all their material is China-adapted, going beyond translation to writing key material in a way that promises and promotes cooperation. They will have visited early and often, thereby identifying areas of common interest and using these to guide both exploratory discussions and the framing of any potential deals.

"Winning companies" will have embraced the concept of extended character due diligence and provided early proofs of good faith to build trust. They will have communicated the extended timelines around negotiation and deal-making to their stakeholders and will be equipped with an authoritative, nontime-sensitive mandate from the latter. This prevents them from making forced errors because of stakeholder pressure. Such companies will further ensure that there is consistency of purpose in their dealings and will prioritize holistic business objectives, early in the discussions with Chinese partners, rather than focusing uniquely on targets, profit centers and financial objectives.

Successful companies will have firmly secured consensus on market positioning, sector dominance, early pricing points and profit targets. They will have mediated the Western desire for early profits with the Chinese preference for low price point entry leading to growth within a market sector and eventual market domination.

They will have the full backing of their board as well as sufficient executive power to keep faith with any promises they make to the Chinese, without reversals of position forced on them by management or stakeholders. Managing stakeholders and boards is a key Chinese talent. No one reaches seniority without showing acute adroitness in this area. Having to reverse positions at the behest of a board, in a negotiation, would involve significant loss of face. Therefore, handling those whose mandate you act upon, is always part of the skill set of any Chinese company leader, board member or senior manager.

We need to show the requisite levels of executive power to function well in China. We need to be very much the ambassador of our company, whilst also acting in a way that is a dignified behavioral counterpoint to our status. We must remember in the vertical Chinese business hierarchy, a CEO has very substantial power and must always act with the dignity befitting a CEO. Alongside this, a CEO in China will often display authentic and warm concern, in this people-centric business culture, for the well-being of all his employees. No-one is considered dispensable in China; people stay, business conditions alter, therefore loyalty to the former is at a premium and constitutes the key business mindset to adopt.

Your handling of people, as a potential partner, will be closely watched and analyzed by the Chinese. It is up to you to ensure that your handling of relationships is never transactional, throw away or peremptory, if you wish to signal relationship finesse and commitment, at the level required for trust-building in China.

If we cannot show that we care about staff and are adept at fostering collegial attitudes and loyalty in those we manage, the Chinese will conclude that we lack the requisite skills for the even more testing business of partnership.

Showing respect and affinity for Chinese values is one of the most meaningful ways to signal our genuine commitment to relationship and partnership. The Chinese like to do business with people who like and respect them. This might seem like a universal preference, to the point of being a truism. Don't we all want this in our business dealings? Well, if we are being rigorously honest, this has become a very secondary concern in our Western business culture, compared to potentially lucrative deals, successes and profitable outcomes. If we were being entirely frank, this has ceased to be a primary concern in our increasingly transactional and pragmatic Western business culture. We now do business in the West, primarily, based on potential success and may take little account of whether we like or entirely trust the potential business partners we are dealing with.

In China, accepting to engage with partners who merely tolerate you for financial gain would harm face and indicate poor judgment. This is highly significant when we remember that, in China, the primary business skill is to be wise and discerning in the critical area of character judgment and business associations.

So, real success in China, often falls to those who have, or who are able to cultivate, knowledge, affection and respect toward China, its culture and its values. We can begin to cultivate an interest in Chinese culture by becoming acquainted with their key thinkers: Confucius, Lao-Tzu the authors of Bing Fa, and not just the ubiquitously quoted Art of War. Chinese business principles are derived from, and heavily informed by these key thinkers, so there is the additional motivating factor whereby knowledge of these thinkers assists us greatly in understanding the success thinking of our Chinese counterparts and allows us to participate in this success.

However adapted surface business conventions and practices become in Chinese business to accommodate partnership with the West, there will always be an underlying mentor in the received wisdom of these great thinkers which internally coaches Chinese people through key moments of their business behavior, decision making and responses.

Awareness of this thinking, particularly in the critical area of relationships, allows you to test your preconceptions and ideas against those of the Chinese. You will ideally become able to accommodate both perspectives harmoniously and fluently. This is the skill of metacognition (Chua 2012), which will be the great skill for success with China in the 21st century and which we can deploy to the benefit of our success goals with this business culture.

Signaling knowledge of these great thinkers, alongside other important aspects of Chinese culture, goes beyond the requisite business protocol exchange, and delivers a powerful message that you have come to participate.

There is another point of differentiation which I have observed between those who succeed in China, and those who do not; it is a fundamental understanding of the responsibilities a Chinese person carries in relation to face, and the breadth of people for whom reputation is carried. In a harmony-seeking business climate, with highly developed self/other integration instilled as a core value from childhood, there is a huge face responsibility burden on each Chinese person. This responsibility extends to family, extended family networks, city, province, country, national pride and the public face of their ethnicity.

Those who succeed within China understand that, for the Chinese, obligations are both a privilege and a duty—a significant and cherished one—but one which is, also, quite heavy to carry. They attempt therefore, as potential partners to the Chinese, to signal their understanding of the breadth and depth of these face commitments. They further seek to show, by every possible means, that they are able and willing to increase reputation by always behaving in ways that protect face. This is a tremendous disposition and skill set for a Westerner to have, in the eyes of the Chinese, who fully understand that such a skill is not one which forms part of our education and cultural values set, in the West.

Displaying such a disposition and skill set, as a Westerner, therefore, shows profound insights into China's relational business culture and gives proof of uncommon levels of business acumen, as defined by the Chinese. This entails demonstrating relationship finesse and people skills, as well as dedication to the mutual benefit, strong reputation and ethical public face of one's partners. Since this is the primary controller of all initiatives, progress and success in China, the Chinese believe that they are utterly secure when they witness this disposition in any potential Western partner. It acts as a catalyst to more assured business discussions, greater goodwill at the negotiating table, and increased wealth. It also assists in both making and protecting deals and ensures that the Chinese work with you to create success at maximum levels.

It further promotes longevity since a thoughtful, culturally sensitive and China-adapted understanding of relationships, is not yet common in many potential Western partners. Such a disposition, therefore, marks you out as desirable and to be solicited. It is the very definition of competitive edge.

The ideal thing is to layer upon this disposition the trust and good faith-enhancing tools from our previous chapters. We must be China-adapted in our ongoing commitment to building trust through our communication styles, knowledge and negotiating approaches, as well as our deal-making and handling of law. If we can achieve this, we will have consolidated our business skills and created a China-adapted disposition. We can then further consolidate these skills into optimum business behavior to engender partnership success.

This will provide the context for building on the trust and security which good partnerships engender, allowing us to create enduring loyalty and lasting success with this people-centric culture, through our command of China-fluent relationship principles and dynamics. By doing this, we guarantee our future with China, since we have signaled that we, too, value relationship and partnership above all else.

# Demonstrating China Fluency

## Key Dos and Don'ts

*To Create Successful Business Relationships in China*

**Do:**
- Prioritize the relationship.
- Take time to understand the Chinese business model.
- Note how the Chinese business model contrasts with your Western business experience and instincts; mediate differences.
- Remember that relationship success is the true business collateral in China.
- Show relationships awareness, concern and attention, at all times.
- Invest more in the business relationship in times of stress.
- See relationships as an indicator of business progress.
- Behave in relationships in ways which promote, and protect, public face.
- Conduct yourself in relationships in ways that promote reputation as well as progress.
- Display relationship "finesse" thoughtfully, carefully and visibly alongside your other business skills.

**Do not:**
- Make relationships simply an accessory to your business skills set;
- Treat relationships casually or with less than consummate respect;
- Neglect the health of the relationship even when under pressure from stakeholders, profit targets or delivery schedules;

- Hurry relationships in China: they take time;
- Act in ways that harm trust, cognitive or affective and the crucial process of bonding;
- Neglect relationship hiccups, challenges or ruptures. These are serious indicators of stalled progress in China;
- Overlook relationships in favor of speedier progress, timelines or pleasing stakeholders;
- See relationship finesse as a soft skill; the Chinese will quickly identify this as a lack of commitment;
- Treat relationships transactionally or in a one-sided manner;

### To Communicate With China

**Do:**

- Use soft, indirect gentle and persuasive styles.
- Aim to communicate respect as well as your message.
- Think about how you are framing your ideas.
- Make bonding an important goal in your communication.
- Deploy metacognition skills by asking yourself how your message will be received.
- Make how you say something as important as what are saying.
- Take your time when framing your ideas and avoid reactive speech.
- Remember the value of silence; this is the hallmark of a mature businessperson in China.
- Respond rather than react; the Chinese value reflection.
- Remember to truly listen. This is a primary business skill in China and needs to be deep.

**Do not:**

- Use direct, dramatic or aggressive speech...*ever*!
- Use humor or idioms; these travel badly across different cultural communication models;
- Be flamboyant or confrontational in your mode of communication;

- Use hurried or poorly thought-out communication in China;
- Show excessive amounts of emotion as the Chinese value moderation and temperance in speech;
- Use communication to draw attention to self as the Chinese value modesty and teamwide communication;
- Criticize someone publicly—this harms face and the health of the business relationship;
- Give public ultimatums; this never works in China and harms business objectives;
- Select a particular individual for either praise or blame. Use teamwide praise and private allocations of responsibility or blame;
- Knee jerk—reflection and maturity of response is what China values;

### To Demonstrate Successful People Skills and Management Styles for China

**Do:**

- View people as your core priority in business with China, not as "human capital."
- Make treating people well as important as business outcomes.
- See people as your greatest asset.
- Observe how holistically the Chinese treat people in their business culture.
- Emulate this holistic approach.
- Show dedication and respect for your own team.
- Discuss your enterprise frequently in terms of its benefits to people.
- Mirror China's vertical hierarchy, with its emphasis on seniority and matching of roles to status, whilst displaying huge dedication to the well-being of your team.
- Show how well people are taken care of in your enterprise.
- Handle accountability and rewards in a way that acknowledges the collective.
- If people have worked hard for your success, even in a secondary role, acknowledge them and visibly reward them.

**Do not:**

- See people as dispensable;
- Treat people in a transactional manner or as mere business assets;
- Isolate an individual for praise, blame or individual accountability;
- Side-line people or make their well-being subordinate to progress or profits;
- Neglect the well-being of your team in the interest of progress; the Chinese view this as poor people-handling;
- Stint on time for your people to eat, rest or recharge as these are viewed as crucial in China;
- Say you are "peopled out" as this concept is alien to the Chinese;
- Self-aggrandize at the expense of your team. China is a collectivist culture and does not value rugged individualism;

## To Negotiate Successfully With China

**Do:**

- Negotiate for mutual benefit.
- Remember the health of your business relationship at all points in the negotiation.
- Take time to explore ideas fully before honing in on negotiating outcomes.
- Make sure that all parties have equal negotiating space.
- Share the floor and allow all voices and representation equal time.
- Frame the negotiation parameters in a way that signals mutual benefit as a goal.
- Match the status of negotiators on both sides.
- Make sure that senior people in your organization frame, open and conclude the negotiation; this is the preferred process in China.
- See the end of the negotiation as a celebration and give it due public face.

**Do not:**

- See negotiation uniquely as a route to realizing business goals;
- Sacrifice relationships to the negotiation process or its progress;
- Avoid being motivated purely by securing results for stakeholders; the Chinese will pick up on this;
- Be effective, but not transactional, in your negotiations; the Chinese can spot the difference;
- Neglect relationship ruptures/pressures; these are indicators that the relationship is failing;
- Use negotiations for your sole advantage;
- Mismatch status in negotiations; remember the Chinese have a vertical business hierarchy;
- Neglect public opportunities to celebrate outcomes;
- Introduce legal ratification too early in the negotiation process or in concluding negotiations;

## To Make Successful Deals With China

**Do:**

- See the deal in terms of mutual benefit.
- See the deal as a vehicle to create shared reputation for both parties.
- View the deal in terms of creating shared face for both parties.
- Consider the benefits to your Chinese partners, their organization, city and province; these matter greatly in China.
- Frame all deals in terms of longevity; the Chinese make deals that *last*.
- Protect the relationship health as you are making the deal.
- Take all opportunities to commit publicly to the deal you and your Chinese partner have made.
- See the deal as a progress marker in your continuing business relationship, not as a destination.
- Consider the deal from all angles, not merely from the viewpoint of ROI.
- Think short, medium and long term in your deal-making; the Chinese always do!

**Do not:**

- Rush deals; hurry harms outcomes in China;
- Neglect the full implications of the deal; it will cause problems later;
- See the deal in terms of your enterprise only;
- Settle for short termism in any deal that you strike;
- Look to profits only; this will defeat the deal in the long term;
- Let stakeholder pressure make you rush the deal;
- Be too rigid in your deal-making. Conceding small points wins big in China;
- Neglect opportunities for joint public face; as the latter protects deals in China;
- Introduce your lawyers too early; legal ratification happens late in Chinese deal-making;
- Fail to celebrate the role of relationship in any deal you make as this is the "real deal";

### To Protect Business Interests and Objectives With China

**Do:**

- Ensure that deals are fully fleshed out before proceeding to contract.
- Use relationships and their progress, to flush out any areas of potential challenge.
- Check that relationships are strong and intact before preparing contracts.
- Embed mutual benefit in all aspects of your contract.
- Ensure that no areas of dissatisfaction remain precontract; China is all or nothing.
- Use lawyers thoughtfully; the Chinese do not hold lawyers in the same regard as us.
- Take time to understand the role of law in China's business model.
- Make the relationship more important than the contract; if anything happens to the former, the latter will not count.

- See the contract as a celebration, not as a protection against contingency or a sanction dispenser in the event of failed delivery.
- Handle the contract phase and use of law with sensitivity and with the intention to protect the relationship, at all costs.
- Handle IPR carefully and sensitively.
- Protect partnerships as well as IPR; the former protects the latter.

**Do not:**
- Lose sight of relationships when making contracts as the former protect the latter;
- Employ harsh tactics or overt robustness at the point of contract—this harms outcomes;
- Display a "yours and mine" attitude: China prefers to deal in mutual benefit;
- Pursue outcomes or ROI in ways that harm the business relationship and then rely on law to repair damage; this does not work in China;
- Neglect tensions at the contract stage; the former harms the latter in this relationship-centric culture;
- Frame contracts in any way that could be perceived as one-sided;
- Use lawyers who are unskilled in Chinese business models, protocols and sensibilities;
- Neglect "shared face" and public celebration of outcomes at the contract stage; this matters enormously to China;

### To Create Mutual Benefit and Reputation in China

**Do:**
- Think collectively; think "We" at all times, since the Chinese do this automatically.
- Seek mutual benefit in how you present and frame business ideas.
- Consider joint face consistently.

- Cultivate ways to enhance your Chinese partner's reputation and face.
- Frame commitment to project and partners thoughtfully and, as often as possible, in public.
- Behave in ways that enhance your Chinese partners' public stock; this cements the partnership.
- Seek to create bonds around character, intention and integrity.
- Seek to show your relationship finesse, often and publicly; allow this to bring benefits to your Chinese partner.
- Respect networks and Guanxi.
- Share skills and knowledge whenever possible; this builds trust.

**Do not:**
- Neglect your partner's face in the way you communicate;
- Pursue one-sided business deals;
- Be overly individualistic in your business behavior; this harms goals;
- Go "off message" about your business partners in public; this has huge face implications in China;
- Publicly criticize a business partner in China or the cultural climate, government or business culture; this will harm your business dialogue;
- Air contentious views publicly as this harms face;
- Express one-sided interests, intentions and views;
- Neglect the well-being of your team or your partner's teams; all success in China is people-centered;
- View your interests as separate to, or more important than, those of your partners; the Chinese will pick up on this and view it as a lack of commitment to the partnership;
- Stint on building bonds, sharing knowledge and competencies and promoting trust in your partners; these factors collectively ensure success in China;

# Conclusion

## Creating Mutual Benefit and Shared Reputation

It is fair to say that shared benefit is seen in the West as emanating from first putting in place successful business arrangements. This is not a primary business goal but, rather, a derivative or consequence. As such, it represents an aspiration; one that is only addressed once the more serious business of reaching profit targets has been secured through negotiation and deal-making leading to intense ratification through legally-binding contracts.

In China, shared reputation and mutual benefit are primary goals and it is expected that they will remain the dominant priority and objective, at all stages of the business process. Reputation and mutual benefit are the central currency of the Chinese business culture. They act as proofs of good faith as well as potent symbols of congruent goals and intentions between parties. They contribute enormously to the successful unfolding of the business process by acting as markers of positive intent, good character and integrity.

In the Chinese conceptual framework, if someone has a proven and sustained commitment to mutual benefit and shared reputation, they will conduct themselves in a relationship-sensitive manner and acquit themselves well within China's relationship-centric culture. This will, in turn, guarantee ultimate success.

More importantly, a commitment to mutual benefit and shared reputation betokens, for China, an understanding of the fundamental principles and protocols of China's business culture. It demonstrates that, although we have come from a more transactional business culture, with a much more process-driven approach to the conduct of our business dealings, we have nonetheless understood the critical importance of putting relationships first, in China.

By making the shift in business emphasis toward relationships, we signal a deep awareness of Chinese sensibilities and values which place the strength of the relationship, and the notion of equal gains for both parties, at the very heart of the business success formula.

When we embrace relationships as a critical priority, we gain China's respect. This, in turn, promotes two states which the Chinese, used to doing business in a people-centric way, find essential pre-requisites to success: security and trust.

We, in the Western business model, tend to understand how to pro-mote security and trust uniquely through proof of professional compe-tencies and delivery capabilities, backed by robust business profiles and adroitly negotiated contracts. This is an exclusively cognitive approach to the building of trust and security. It neglects the affective dimension which is so important to potential business partners in China, and which is reflected for them in the health of the business relationship itself.

The Chinese, on the other hand, build security and trust through the affective route, whilst securing the cognitive element of trust through business competencies checks. Such checks happen early in the business process and are then relegated to a secondary position, whilst the crucial next stage of building relationships and affective trust is carried out. In China, trust and security are engendered through a commitment to, and expert handling of, the business relationship; this, in turn, facilitates all success creation.

When we prove that we are adept at participating in this relation-ship-centric business model, we signal a commitment to the very pillars and fundamentals of success-creation in China. We must further con-solidate this by showing a profound, and authentic, connection to the cultural values which underpin this people-centric, collectivist business model. In doing so, we signal a degree of China-fluency which empow-ers partnerships and fuels success-creation. Even more importantly, our emphasis on relationships ensures robust loyalty from, and enduring longevity of association with, our Chinese partners, clients and collabo-rators. In the increasingly transactional, volatile and unpredictable land-scape of global business, there can be no more enduringly attractive or solicited goal.

# References

Brant, R. 2021. "China Census: Data Shows Slowest Population Growth in Decades." *BBC News*. Available at www.bbc.co.uk/news/world-asia-china-57067180 (accessed June 10, 2021).

Chakravarthy, B., and D. Yau. 2016. "Global Contenders from China: What are their Challenges?" *Institute for Management Development* (IMD). Available at www.imd.org/research-knowledge/articles/global-contenders-from-china-what-are-their-challenges/ (accessed June 10, 2021).

Chen, M. 2001. *Inside Chinese Business: A Guide for Managers Worldwide*. Boston, Mass: Harvard Business Review Press.

Ching, M.K. 2009. *CFO Guide to doing Business in China*. Singapore: John Wiley & Sons (Asia).

Chua, R.Y.J. June 19, 2012. "Building Effective Business Relationships in China." MIT Sloan Management Review. Available at www.sloanreview.mit.edu/article/building-effective-business-relationships-in-china/ (accessed June 10 2021).

Clyne, M. 1995. *Inter-cultural Communication at Work: Cultural Values in Discourse*. Cambridge: Cambridge University Press

Confucius. 1998. *The Original Analects: Sayings of Confucius and his Successors*, E. Bruce Brooks and A. Taeko Brooks (trans/eds), (Translations from the Asian Classics), New York: Columbia University Press.

Csikszentmihalyi, M. Summer, 2020 (Ed). "Confucius." *The Stanford Encyclopaedia of Philosophy*. Available at https://plato.stanford.edu/entries/confucius/ (accessed May 12, 2021).

De Monte, B.L. 2004. *Chinese Etiquette & Ethics in Business*. 2nd edn. New York: McGraw-Hill.

Fisher, R., W. Ury., and B. Patton. 2011. *Getting to Yes: Negotiating Agreement Without Giving In*. 3rd edn. New York: Penguin.

Gascoigne, B. 2003 *The Dynasties of China: A History*. London: Robinson.

Goh, B.C. 1996. *Negotiating with the Chinese*. Brookfield, VT: Dartmouth Publishing.

Herholdt, J., ed. 2012. *People Management Strategy in Organisations: Articles from Human Capital Review*, 1st edn. Johannesburg: Knowres Publishing.

Iritani, E. September 9, 2004. "Great Idea but Don't Quote Him." *Los Angeles Times*. Available at www.latimes.com/archives/la-xpm-2004-sep-09-fi-deng9-story.html (accessed June 10, 2021).

McNeilly, M.R. 2012. *Sun Tzu and the Art of Business: Six Strategic Principles for Managers*. New York: Oxford University Press.

Xiao, R. 2009. "Between Adapting and Shaping: China's Role in Asian Regional Cooperation." *Journal of Contemporary China* 18, no. 59, pp. 303—320.

Reuvid, J., ed. 2011. *Business insights: China*, 2nd edn. London: Kogan Page.

Rudman, S.T. 2006. *The Multinational Corporation in China: Controlling Interests*. Oxford: Blackwell

Scollon, R., and S. Wong Scollon. 2001. *Intercultural Communication: A Discourse Approach*. 2nd edn. Oxford: Blackwell.

Sinha, K. 2008. *China's Creative Imperative: How Creativity is Transforming Society and Business in China*. Singapore; Hoboken, NJ: John Wiley & Sons (Asia).

Spence, J.D. 2012. *The Search for Modern China*. 3rd edn. New York: W. W. Norton & Company.

Stuttard, J.B. 2000. *The New Silk Road: Secrets of Business Success in China Today*. New York: John Wiley & Sons.

Turley, J. 2010. *Connecting with China*. Chichester: John Wiley & Sons Ltd.

Ury, W. 1993. *Getting Past No: Negotiating in Difficult Situations*. New York: Bantam Books.

Ury, W. 2000. *The Third Side: Why We Fight and How We Can Stop*. New York: Penguin Books.

Ury, W. 2007. *The Power of a Positive No: Save The Deal Save The Relationship and Still Say No*. New York: Bantam Books.

# About the Author

**Joan Turley** began her career as an academic specializing in modern languages, having previously won The French Government Medal for her undergraduate language studies. Having acquired a master's degree through the French postgraduate system, Joan engaged in a lifelong fascination with the rigors of relating well to other cultures for work and business. After her PhD studies, she specialized in the application of English for the International Business community, followed by three years at a global strategic research company applying cultural values to the analysis of competitive information.

For the past 10 years, Joan has specialized in applying her extensive cultural skills to enhancing her clients' business performance. Her work seeks to promote success, mutual benefit and empathy through effective intercultural dialogue between Western clients and China across business, education, finance, media, and government.

Joan Turley provides clear signposts and compelling insights to help those working with China to understand the value of relationships in this business culture and the importance of people as key elements in making business flourish. Her extremely powerful books will unlock your ability to build working relationships for enterprise success with China.

# Index

Accountability, 1, 8, 23, 41–43, 62, 63
Adversity, 57–58
Affective trust, 9, 27
*The Art of War,* 57, xxi

China–adapted relationship skills, xiii
China, enterprise success
   business culture, xvi
   communication
      culturally adapted skills development, 16–20
      dos and don'ts, 70–71
      east/west communication norms, 13–15
      parameters of, 14
      styles, 20
conflict resolution
   communication strategies for, 54–55
   east/west perspectives, 49–51
   through respect and entente, 56–59
   through shared vision, 52–54
creating relationships, xvii–xxii
creation
   contrasting east/west perspectives, 61–63
   nurturance, 64–68
deal protection, 39–40
   dos and don'ts, 74–75
   keeping deals safe, 40–44
   relationships protection, 39–40
deals making
   contrasting east/west cultural perspectives, 29–31
   dos and don'ts, 73–74
   successful deals development, 31–37
defined, 61
fluency, 69–76

negotiation
   contrasting east/west attitudes, 21–24
   dos and don'ts, 72–73
   optimum china-adapted styles, 24–28
overview, ix–xvii
relationships, 1–2
   creation, xvii–xxii
   dos and don'ts, 69–70
   making, 4–12
   successful handling, 3–4
Cognitive trust, 9, 27
Commonality, lack of, 51
Communication
   culturally adapted skills development, 16–20
   dos and don'ts, 70–71
   east/west communication norms, 13–15
   parameters of, 14
   strategies for conflict resolution, 54–55
   styles, 20
Conflict avoidance, 47–48
Conflict, origins of, 51–52
Conflict resolution, 4
   communication strategies for, 54–55
   east/west perspectives, 49–51
   handling, 49
   through respect and entente, 56–59
   through shared vision, 52–54
Connection, xix
Cultural metacognition, 11

Deal protection, 39–40
   dos and don'ts, 74–75
   implementation phase, 43
   keeping deals safe, 40–44
   relationships protection, 39–40

Deals making
    contrasting east/west cultural
        perspectives, 29–31
    dos and don'ts, 73–74
    successful deals development, 31–37
Dignity, 50
Disparity, 51

Empathy, 53
Entente, 56–59

Holistic integration, 35

Intellectual property rights (IPR), 8, 40
Intercultural conflict, 53
IPR. *See* Intellectual property rights
    (IPR)

Knowledge protection, 44–46

Law, 39–41

Management styles, 71–72
McDonald's, 56–57
Metacognition, 11, 22–24, 28, 53, 67
Moments of conflict, 55
Mutual benefit, 7, 10, 29, 35, 50, 54,
    64, 75–78

Negotiation
    contrasting east/west attitudes,
        21–24
    dos and don'ts, 72–73
    optimum china-adapted styles,
        24–28

Optimal negotiation, 50

*pàn* (making judgment), 24
Paying attention, 23
People-centric culture, 15, 58, 68,
    ix–x
People handling, 65–66
People skills, 2–3

dos and don'ts, 71–72
Performance, 1–2
Project management, 42
Public communication, 14

Relationship-centric business culture,
    5, 53, x, xi–xii
Relationships, 1–2
    building, 36
    creation, xvii–xxii
    dos and don'ts, 69–70
    making, 4–12
    preservation, 17
    protection, 39–40
    successful handling, 3–4
Reputation, 15, 23, 30–31, 65–66
Respect, 56–59

Sealing the deal, 39
Securing the trade, 39
Security, 30
Shared reputation, 15, 29, 75–78
Shared vision, 52–54
Soft communication, 13–14
Soft skills, 2
Stakeholder management, 65
Success creation
    contrasting east/west perspectives,
        61–63
    nurturance, 64–68

*tán* (discussion), 24
Thinking, 29
Tone, communication, 13, 47
Trust, 61, 78
    building, 1, 8, 9, 27, 64
    key element, 44

Western business culture, 25, 41, 55,
    56, 66
Western business model, 5, 9, 78
Western business negotiations, 41
*wēiii,* 36
Win/win, 26, 28, 35, 45, 47, 54, 57
"Winning companies," 64–65

## OTHER TITLES IN THE INTERNATIONAL BUSINESS COLLECTION

S. Tamer Cavusgil, Manchester Business School;
Michael Czinkota, Georgetown; and
Gary Knight, Willamette University, Editors

- *The Chinese Market Series* by Danai Krokou
- *Trading With China* by Danai Krokou
- *The Chinese e-Merging Market* by Danai Krokou
- *The Chinese Market* by Danai Krokou
- *Creative Solutions to Global Business Negotiations, Third Edition* by Claude Cellich
- *Exporting* by Laurent Houlier and John Blaskey
- *Global Trade Strategies* by Michel Borgeon and Claude Cellich
- *Doing Business in Germany* by Andra Riemhofer
- *Major Business and Technology Trends Shaping the Contemporary World* by Hamid Yeganeh

## Concise and Applied Business Books

The Collection listed above is one of 30 business subject collections that Business Expert Press has grown to make BEP a premiere publisher of print and digital books. Our concise and applied books are for…

- Professionals and Practitioners
- Faculty who adopt our books for courses
- Librarians who know that BEP's Digital Libraries are a unique way to offer students ebooks to download, not restricted with any digital rights management
- Executive Training Course Leaders
- Business Seminar Organizers

Business Expert Press books are for anyone who needs to dig deeper on business ideas, goals, and solutions to everyday problems. Whether one print book, one ebook, or buying a digital library of 110 ebooks, we remain the affordable and smart way to be business smart. For more information, please visit www.businessexpertpress.com, or contact sales@businessexpertpress.com.